ND FEMALESE

Born in 1981 in New York to an American father and Scottish mother, Jean Hannah Edelstein is a relationship expert for the twenty-first century, with a signature style that combines New York sass and British wit. Jean lives in London, where she works as a freelance journalist, having written in print and online for the *Guardian*, *Observer*, *Independent*, *Independent on Sunday*, *New Statesman* and *Sunday Times*, on topics ranging from sex to politics to literature. Jean also appears as a commentator on radio and television, and blogs on relationship matters at www.himglishandfemalese.com.

HIMGLISH AND FEMALESE

*Why women don't get why
men don't get them*

Jean Hannah Edelstein

This paperback edition published by Arrow Books 2010

10 9 8 7 6 5 4 3 2 1

First published in Great Britain in 2009 by Preface Publishing

Arrow Books
20 Vauxhall Bridge Road,
London, SW1V 2SA

An imprint of The Random House Group

www.rbooks.co.uk

Addresses for companies within The Random House Group Limited
can be found at www.randomhouse.co.uk

The Random House Group Limited Reg. No. 954009

A CIP catalogue record for this book is available from the British Library

ISBN 978 1 84809 172 6

The Random House Group Limited supports The Forest Stewardship Council (FSC),
the leading international forest certification organisation. All our titles that are printed
on Greenpeace-approved FSC-certified paper carry the FSC logo. Our paper
procurement policy can be found at www.rbooks.co.uk/environment

Typeset by Palimpsest Book Production Limited,
Grangemouth, Stirlingshire

Printed and bound in Great Britain by CPI Bookmarque, Croydon, CR0 4TD

To all the men who said, 'Please don't put me in your book.'

Contents

Introduction

The first boy I ever loved was also three years old: Alex and I went to nursery school together, where we whiled away many a happy quarter of an hour – we had brief attention spans – hammering away at blocks of wood on the classroom woodworking table. In retrospect, this seems like it must have been very dangerous, but I guess in 1985 there were no health and safety rules that precluded three-year-olds from wielding chisels.

Anyway, in addition to sharing my precocious passion for sawing things, Alex had many other characteristics that made him, overall, a fine young man to love. While it is true that he was extremely short, I was too, at the time. But Alex had big blue eyes, hair the colour and texture of the strands of silk in an ear of corn, and dimples. And he had an extensive wardrobe of corduroy dungarees in a range of earth tones and a quite solid grasp of the niceties of toilet training. In the world of nursery school, I think that any of the small girls in our class would have agreed with me: Alex was pretty money.

But the thing that made me really love Alex, the thing that made our relationship extra-special, was that he had a speech impediment. At least, I thought he had a speech impediment. When I consider the situation in retrospect, it seems possible that Alex just spoke like an average three-year-old and I interpreted this as a pathological problem – you may not be surprised to learn that I was a bit of a chatterbox. In fact, perhaps English wasn't Alex's mother tongue and he was actually speaking fluent German when I thought he was speaking fluent gibberish. But of course, at the time, none of these possible explanations for his vocal shortcomings occurred to me. I was gallant for my trio of years and I latched on to Alex because I saw an opportunity for me to play a special role in his life. Feeling very noble, I assumed, without any kind of explicit consent from Alex, the role of his translator. I was scrupulous about my responsibility to convey to the other kids, and the adults, information that, now that I think about it, often probably had nothing to do with what Alex was actually trying to say.

Poor little Alex. We went our separate ways when we turned five and it was time for us to attend kindergarten, and I never saw him again. I seem to recall my mother telling me that his family had moved away, but now I wonder if in fact Alex's parents put their son in a new school so that he would at least have a chance to learn to speak for himself before my domineering influence stunted his personal development for good. What if, to this day, he is simply struck dumb around women, waiting for them to speak on his behalf? I feel a little bit guilty.

But only a very little bit. Because when I think about this further, it occurs to me that I might have indeed been doing Alex a great service. I must have prepared him well for one of the most basic and common and challenging experiences of male adult life: having women try to interpret what he says and often getting it wrong; feeling a bit powerless and unable to understand why it is, exactly, that members of the opposite sex often cannot seem to understand the very simple and straightforward things that he says and does, the clear messages that he is sending.

Yes, in fact, I think that I can say with confidence that my relationship with little Alex was just another example of a long-held tradition of the human race that crosses generations and cultural boundaries. Men and women have both long been perplexed by the opposite sex and tried to mitigate that perplexity by attempting to employ their own interpretations and assumptions to explain or justify the other's confusing behaviour. Although it is not a tradition that is, or should be, particularly beloved, it is among our most enduring ones and cuts across both genders: women have been trying to figure men out, and vice versa, since time began. We can't seem to help ourselves, even though sometimes it can have a quite deleterious effect on our lives. It's not entirely a bad thing, of course: if men and women did understand each other perfectly, there would be far fewer artists in the world and a lot more accountants. But sometimes, when it's a matter of going about your daily life and not a matter of composing an opera, the sense that boys and girls are sometimes chalk and cheese can be more than a little bit frustrating.

Because we know ourselves better than we know anyone else, it is only natural that members of both sexes tend to believe that our default behaviours make perfect sense and that it is the opposite sex with the problem. We feel safe to assume that they are the ones who are odd and inexplicable and foreign and sometimes just downright uncivilised. But this is a lazy kind of conclusion to draw, an easy way out: why try to understand the other half when you can be smug and confident in your supposition that they are irrational?

It is a strategy that many people have used for a long time, but with limited success, which is why, within the following pages, I am going to propose that we knock it off. It is fine to accept that men and women may think and behave differently in various circumstances. But that is no excuse for writing off comprehension of the opposite sex as an impossible task: in the long run, making the effort makes our own lives less stressful, saving us, ideally, from quite a lot of unnecessary weeping.

Before we crack on with this exciting undertaking, however, I do feel that it is important to note that while this kind of squinting and brow-furrowing when considering the opposite sex may be a fairly universal phenomenon, the differences between the sexes aren't always. This is not only because of general variances in cultural trends but also because of the sporadic evolution of mixed-gender relations over the course of history in different places and communities. It is a process that has always been dynamic but which has not necessarily always been progressive: assuming that we have it better than our ancestors can be an over-simplification. As we head at a rapid clip into the second decade of the third millennium, it is clear that in many respects inter-gender relationships have never been less tangled up in red tape – but, at the same time, that our relative freedom has created new conflicts and misunderstandings and, in some cases, challenges and limitations that have defied expectations by becoming endemic.

So what does our project here encompass? Well, in the chapters that follow, I've broken key issues down into a number of different categories, running the gamut of male–female relations and interactions from the very basics of communication to the most advanced complexities of love and life. I've done some research on your behalf, checking out what science has had to say about men and women recently and comparing these conclusions against what I have observed, and what people I've interviewed have experienced, in order to deduce what the contemporary trends of gender relations are.

In order to more precisely illustrate some of the phenomena that we will be discussing herein, I have drafted in some assistance in the form of two fictional characters. In the following pages, you will meet the plucky Alice Femalese and the spirited Jonathan Himglish. They are a young couple of indeterminate age (I believe they fall somewhere within the 18–34 demographic) who have been together for an indeterminate amount of time and have a varying – sometimes indeterminate, even! – degree of difficulty when it comes to understanding each other just like, well, the rest of us.

Isn't this exciting? Oh, my friends, it is. But before we get properly stuck in, you also need to be properly introduced to me, your guide for the spectacular adventure that we are about to embark on. You are probably thinking, right now, who exactly is this Jean Hannah Edelstein person, and how exactly is she qualified to explain to me these mysteries that she herself has just pointed out are as old as the hills?

Who I am, in fact, is a person not entirely unlike you: a woman who is navigating the trials and travails of living and working alongside members of the opposite sex in an epoch that is quite unlike any that has come along previously (which is, of course, pretty standard for epochs – we're not *that* special). I, too, spend far too much time trying to speculate about what messages men are trying to convey to me, only to often find that I am way off the mark because I have made the cardinal error of assuming that they are always communicating in the same way that I do.

Like you, I fall in and out of love with men from time to time and wonder why and what and how it happens; I, too, negotiate tricky domestic issues. I worry about sex and I struggle to negotiate the difficult problems that crop up when I try to get along being a woman in a man's world – and, sometimes, in dealing with men when the roles are reversed and they find themselves in mine. Sure, I am far from the first person to write on this topic, but the rapid evolution of society – particularly over the last decade – means that there are a lot of fresh and new ways for men and women to clash over what is, in essence, an ancient conflict.

And thus, I'm here to offer you a thorough examination of the issues that dog our everyday lives from the front lines, so to speak. I didn't purchase a Ph.D. on the Internet in order to do this; rather, I have learned from my experiences, from the experiences of others, and from the immense glut of information on this rich topic that the media, in all its various forms, constantly bombards us with, claiming to freshly explain human behaviour to us on a daily basis, whether it's based on careful scientific research or hearsay or surveys conducted by companies that manufacture birth control pills. We have so much information that it is easy to feel overloaded, to feel resigned to the fact that there is no hope of even beginning to understand the half of the population with sex chromosomes different to our own. It is easiest of all to just accept defeat.

I do have sincere sympathy for those of you who feel defeated – I, too, have thrown up my hands once in a while and sworn that I was giving up ever trying to understand the opposite sex. But I have never been able to commit to such a policy for more than five minutes. Resigning yourself to considering men or women inexplicable is tantamount to accepting that you are incapable of being civilised. I don't think that is acceptable, and I don't think that you do either.

So in order for us all to avoid being unacceptable, I am taking the reins and making the project a little bit easier for you. I have boiled the big questions down into one handy volume that you can carry in your handbag, read on the train, discuss with your friends. If you feel especially confident – and I hope that you will, after you finish reading this – you can even leave this book in a tempting, suggestive fashion on a coffee table or nightstand. Your boyfriend or husband might just be moved to pick it up when you've left the room to slip into something a little more comfortable, and he, too, might find that he appreciates the opportunity to become a little more enlightened.

My approach, you see, is an even-handed one: both women and men are sometimes at fault for being difficult and strange towards the opposite sex; neither women nor men can be consistently blamed for the awkwardness and misunderstanding. So no one is let off the hook. Like it or not, unless we join strict, gender-segregated religious orders, we do have to live with each other, and making half of the population out to be scapegoats or suggesting that one half must constantly manipulate the other is simply not the way forward. Unless the way forward involves you being rather bitter and maybe even a bit lonely.

Now, there are two more small points that I feel I must emphasise before we move onwards and upwards. First of all, I am going to make quite a lot of sweeping generalisations in these pages, as one must do when writing a book that engages in a broad discussion of one of the world's most complicated topics. Sometimes the generalisations will annoy you. 'This does not precisely reflect my personal experience,' you may find yourself thinking, furrowing your brow. 'What is she talking about? This is poppycock!'

It is just not a good idea for you to get all agitated like that. Please realise, instead, that in this volume I am not seeking to offer a panacea for all of the troubles of contemporary gender relations and the associated issues of discrimination and anger and the like. That's a giant task that I'd like to think I might be able to play a small part in at some point in my career, but it is a task that no one woman can shoulder entirely. Nor should any of us be expected to. Here, instead, I am hoping to offer you a bit of elucidation of some of those things that you've never quite been able to put your finger on, combined with some food for thought that will give you interesting things to talk about with your friends, your family, your colleagues – and, even if you have to do it via the stealthy techniques described above, I hope that this book will offer you something, once you are feeling quite brave, to share with your partners.

Ultimately, of course, all forms of relationships between men and women are unique and special (we will discuss this more thoroughly throughout the book) and I don't see my role here as one that is dictatorial so much as it is, I hope, suggestive, stimulating, and, once in a while, provocative – albeit never gratuitous. And I am well aware that although my thoughts on these issues are being published in old-school book form in the first instance, it is being published in an era of interactive media. So let's interact: if you do disagree with me, or you think that I've missed something, or you have questions, or you would generally like to engage in further conversation about some of the topics that I touch on here, then I hope that you will feel free to send me an email, to jean@himglishandfemalese.com. I will write back.

My second caveat is this: at heart, this book is a work of non-fiction. I am happy to admit, however, that I have changed names and details in many of the stories within, sometimes in order to make an illustration work better and sometimes simply in order to make my anecdotes suffi-ciently ambiguous so that the people who have inspired some of my best tales from the front lines of relating (thanks, folks) get to maintain their dignity. And also because I would prefer that no one sues me. Actually, it is mostly because I would prefer that no one sues me.

Are you ready to get started? And by 'get started', I mean: are you ready to change the way that you relate to the oppo-site sex for ever, and for the better? You know you want to.

1

Communication: Himglish, Femalese, and Other Ways We Get Our Wires Crossed

Debates have raged for time immemorial about the crucial differences in the ways that men and women communicate. A wide variety of reasons for these differences are cited, without, of course, any kind of definitive conclusion being reached. Resolution is rather difficult, I am sure, in light of the fact that representatives of both sexes are engaged in this particular debate. We can't agree about how men and women communicate differently because we can't communicate with each other. Isn't it just the very catchiest of Catch-22s?

Quite simply there are a multitude of opinions on the matter. A selection, a variety, a myriad, a plethora.

Or, as I might say if I was a man writing this book, a shedload.

One school of thought holds that women utter far more words than men because, much like our magnificent bosoms, the language centres in our brains are better developed than those which our male counterparts possess. If it is indeed the case, one might well surmise that is in part because, back in the days of yore in which we ('we' being humankind, that is) were hunters and gatherers, women did lots of chatting when they were out collecting plant-based food (wouldn't you need to gossip to pass the time during the tedious process of collecting seeds? I know I would) while the strong, silent menfolk trampled their manly way through the forests, stalking woolly mammoths or tigers or dinosaurs for a nice Sunday roast – the pursuit of which, of course, would only have been derailed by idle chit-chat which might have scared the prey off.

Of course, other very intelligent people who have studied human development from other perspectives have said that this is nonsense. Subscribers to another key school of thought maintain that the differences in the way that gender defines our use of language come down to social conditioning. We simply expect women to say more because of generations (and generations, and generations) of social and cultural gender stereotyping that all of the feminism in the world has not, it seems, been able to shift. In any case, regardless of the actual grounds of our assumptions, we tend to be consistent in our expectations: when we are at our laziest when it comes to generalising about gender and communication, we anticipate that our daughters will be chatty to a fault, while we expect that our sons, like their fathers, will be quiet and taciturn and most comfortable communicating through a simple system of monosyllables and the occasional grunt.

For these reasons, women take their responsibility for communication so seriously that sometimes – OK, whenever possible – they even speak on behalf of their male friends and relatives. I, personally, have found that this is in particular a very useful technique when a consensus needs to be reached – something which I am sure that all of my ex-boyfriends will be happy to confirm. But it is not always quite so effective when a particular circumstance actually requires that a range of opinions needs to be surveyed. Indeed, my own experience has shown that although I may know in my heart of hearts that I am always right, sometimes the men in my life are happier for me to at least pretend that I am not totally inflexible.

Now, just to clarify, it can be argued that this assumption that girls talk more than boys is not just something that is based on rumour and innuendo. For example, I seem to recall from my Introduction to Psychology course at university (I knew it would come in handy eventually) that younger brothers of older sisters are likely to begin speaking at a slightly older-than-average age than the, er, average child, simply because there's no reason for the wee chaps to give it a shot on their own when they can depend on the women in their lives – their big sisters, their mothers, their talkative girlfriends at nursery school – to serve as their official spokeswomen. No offense to my gentleman readers, but I think that we can all agree that this is rather lazy of the wee chaps. Although, on second thought, maybe we should regard it as marvellously efficient. After all, it permits you boys to devote the time that your big sisters spend negotiating televison privileges and fish finger dinners with your parents to the development of your obsession with supporting the sports teams that will give you reason to get up in the morning for the rest of your lives.

You could study this for a lifetime (er, lots of people do, of course. They are called social scientists), but for our purposes here – a bit of enlightenment, some food for thought – we're going to consider what I believe are the four most important ways in which men and women differ in their use of language.

Dearest gentlemen readers, here is a bulleted list of them for your reference, because (as I will explain shortly in greater detail, which your gender may make you inclined to skim), that is exactly how you like it:

1. Direct versus indirect speech
2. Questions
3. Tonality
4. Disclosing and eliciting personal information

Darling lady readers, I will now go on and carefully expand these four points, in keeping with our tendency to prefer things to be detailed and long-winded and explained in a thorough manner.

It is important to note that actual scientists have spent hours working in research labs substantiating these key differences. I admire their dedication, and indeed their admirable applications of the scientific method. I, on the other hand, found that it was possible to test these four assumptions not through science but simply through dedicated hours of eavesdropping on random couples attempting to have private conversations in restaurants, on buses, at the supermarket, in queues – despite my intrusive, lurking presence. And I also pretended to go to the ladies' a lot when I was out on dates with perfectly nice men so that I could take copious notes. Sorry, random couples. Heartfelt apologies, perfectly nice men (who think I have an abnormally small bladder). But I'm not too sorry: after all, my nosiness and note-taking was for the service of the greater good, even if I did destroy the atmosphere in circumstances that could have otherwise led to some very romantic interludes.

Direct versus indirect speech

Various studies conducted by people in lab coats have found on a number of occasions that the average man utters as much as a staggering sixty-five per cent fewer words than the average woman on the average day. (Statistics on how often men make meaningful grunty noises in lieu of uttering actual words are, alas, not available. I will gladly welcome applications from female readers who would like to volunteer to collect mumble-data from their male partners for the second edition of this book.) With this kind of strict limitation, I think it makes sense that men employ more direct forms of speech than their female counterparts – much like living with limited funds requires one not to indulge in excessive spending, you don't want to mess around with superfluous adjectives and fancy metaphors if you are dealing with such a tiny supply of words.

Women, on the other hand, seem to have utterances to spare, and thus we often slosh our word-wealth about with the kind of careless insouciance that is usually associated with the manner in which celebrity heiresses dole out pink champagne. This approach will often extend to written communication as well – when left to our own devices, women tend to have far higher rates of waffling when it comes to writing. In fact, had a man written this book, I rather suspect, it wouldn't be a book: it would cover two sides of an A4 sheet of paper. Or, if written by an especially pithy gent, a Post-it note.

Because of this intrinsic conflict between being short- and long-winded, we often find ourselves in circumstances where men and women who are supposedly speaking the same language can express the same thoughts in completely different ways. One could say that in any given language, there are two distinct dialects: men speak 'Himglish,' women speak 'Femalese'. To understand better how this works – or doesn't work at all – I find it handy to eavesdrop on a few conversations between Jonathan and Alice.

(Jonathan's mother is coming to visit; both Jonathan and Alice are aware that the living room needs a bit of a spit and polish.)

Jonathan: We need to clean the lounge. My mother is coming to visit.

(Femalese interpretation: My mother hates you and thinks that you are a slovenly housekeeper.)

Alice: Jonathan! The living room is in a shocking condition! I cannot bear to look at it anymore, it fills my heart with woe. Why do you leave your trainers by the sofa like this? Do you think that the room is a rubbish tip? Do you not understand how mortifying it will be for both of us if your mother sees our home in this disastrous state?

(Himglish translation: We need to clean the house. Especially you.)

(Jonathan and Alice are selecting outfits to wear to a dinner party.)

Alice: You wear that shirt a lot, don't you? You never wear the pink shirt that I got you for your birthday.

(Himglish translation: Change your shirt, dude.)

Jonathan: I like this shirt.

(Femalese interpretation: I dislike the shirt that you got me for my birthday and my refusal to wear it this evening is evidence not only of my poor taste in clothing but also of a general disregard for your feelings and our relationship; I am attempting to tell you that I want to break up with you.)

Alice: Do you think that I should wear this gorgeous new purple top that I picked up yesterday while shopping during my lunch break, or should I wear the red one that I wore to your brother's birthday party?

(Himglish translation: I want to wear my new purple top. Agree with me.)

Jonathan: I like that red top.

(Femalese interpretation: The purple top makes you look fat. I no longer love you.)

(Jonathan and Alice are doing the weekly grocery shop.)

Jonathan: Do we need more dish detergent?

(Femalese intepretation: I have not been pulling my weight in terms of housekeeping duties and am thus uncertain about our present levels of washing-up liquid.)

Alice: Do you think we do?

(Himglish translation: You don't do the dishes nearly enough, jerk.)

Of course, conversations in Himglish and Femalese don't just happen between couples like Jonathan and Alice; the languages are employed in non-relationship contexts as well. I give you the following cases in point:

Working

Himglish: You're fired.

Femalese: I feel that our goals are no longer in accordance and I regret to have to say that you will want to start seeking alternative employment, perhaps in another field in which your particular skill set might be more suitable.

Himglish: Did you file the documents?

Femalese: Remember those documents that I gave to you a few days ago? Oh, you do? You know, I have been wondering what happened to them.

Dating

Himglish: Would you like to go out for a drink with me?

Femalese: I seem not to have any plans for Thursday night. Woe is me. I suppose I will just have to stay at home and wash my hair, or watch television while eating ice cream out of a tub, unless somehow, totally unexpectedly, someone offers me a better option.

Himglish: I fancy you.

Femalese: You are very smart and talented. And tall. Did I mention that I like smart, talented, tall men? They really are my favourite type of man. Yes, I really enjoy them.

Himglish: I want to have sex with you.

Femalese: Good heavens! Look at the time. I seem to have missed the last bus. I'd better sleep over, here, in your bed. Oh, that is kind of you to offer to sleep on the couch, but it would be far too rude of me to inconvenience you like that. Hm, I really need to change into something more comfortable. Can I borrow a T-shirt to sleep in? I seem to be wearing some very brief and lacy underwear. I hope you will not be offended if you inadvertently catch a glimpse.

At this point it is also important to mention the issue of being fake (which, you will not be surprised, we shall explore in more depth a bit later on in this book, in the chapter on sex). Women are famous for their habit of being false about their true feelings in conversation, in contrast to men, who are better known for their tendecy to either tell bold-faced lies or be painfully honest. (I went out for some time with a man who fell so squarely in the latter category that I eventually had to beg him to stop giving me his opinion on anything unless I made a very specific request to hear it.) Thanks to our facility for using language in a vague, extensive way, coupled with the social pressure many of us feel to be nice at all costs and avoid conflict, women often find that being at least a little bit fake often feels much easier than truth-telling, even whilst the men in their lives look on and observe the white lies and are filled with nothing but despair at how much it complicates both romantic and platonic relationships (for surely it is the men closest to us who are the best at detecting faking, followed by our mothers).

And thus: even if you remember nothing else about the ways in which members of the opposite sex communicate, I suggest that it is best for you to keep this particular tenet close to your heart (or, if you prefer, written on a little card that you carry around in your wallet): women speak in code, and men do not. Understanding the separation of the two approaches is important, but it is also quite diffi-cult to do. Rather, it is far too often the case that we assume that the opposite sex speaks in the same way that we do; as a result, we tune our ears to listen to the kind of meaning that we ourselves would use the same words to mean. This is a cardinal error! The result of this kind of thinking tends to be the ensuing of chaos: women attempt to deconstruct men's simple sentences and infuse them with meaning that absolutely isn't intended; men take what women are saying at face value, and thus fail to comprehend the crucial underlying messages. Next stop? Weeping.

So. The lessons here are quite simple. Are you ready?

Girls: just because a man remarks that he also loves your favourite book doesn't mean you should start shopping for a wedding dress. It means that he loves your favourite book also. That's nice, but it's just a book. Although it can be very hard, for the sake of your self-preservation, I urge you to try to control your excitement.

Boys: when your long-distance girlfriend mentions that she is taking a business trip that could possibly include a detour through your town, then she is saying that she wants you to invite her to come and see you, rather than have you remark upon what an astonishing coincidence it is that she is going to be passing so near. When women make tangential remarks like that, it is called a hint; please, my dear gentlemen, learn to take one.

Questions

The particular, perhaps peculiar, tangential way that women talk is most apparent when we are asking questions. For women, questioning can take many forms. And one of the most popular forms is, in fact, similar to the way that men speak when they are making a statement. This is, of course, fiendishly confusing to men and, I would imagine, often gives them headaches. Poor boys.

Take, for example, a simple scenario in which the rubbish needs to be taken out. Jonathan and Alice struggle with this one. When Jonathan wants Alice to do bin duty, he says something along the lines of 'Would you take the rubbish out, please?' This puts Alice in a small funk, because taking the rubbish out is smelly and unpleasant and surely not something that women's liberation requires her to do every week in order to maintain her fervent belief in gender equality. But because Alice is an upstanding lady and not some kind of ridiculous princess (no one likes a ridiculous princess, girls) she will do it, since saying 'no' would be strange and obtuse. And thus the chore is done, and efficiently so.

But unfortunately, Jonathan tends not to take notice of the overflowing bin quite as often as he might. Alice often feels that she must take it upon herself to ask him to take care of it. But the chances that she will directly ask him to do this are low – not only does it not come naturally, but she is wary of being labelled a nag, which is definitely amongst the most offensive stereotypes with which a lady can be lumbered. In order to avoid being bossy, therefore, Alice is more likely to couch her request in a statement, rather that putting it to Jonathan as a question. Thus, Alice remarks, 'I see the rubbish needs to be taken out,' which is intended to be a direction, rather than a mere observation; unfortunately, however, only the man who is aware that women speak in code will respond correctly and convey the bag to the bin. Jonathan is not amongst this elite group.

Being a rather more literally minded bloke, Jonathan will observe the overflowing pile of trash, and agree with his lovely Alice that it is indeed time for it to go. And then he will plug his iPod back in and continue to drink his beer. And then Alice will be annoyed with him for not understanding what she was saying. And then she'll end up nagging him about it – doing exactly what she was trying to avoid in the first place by using indirect language to direct Jonathan to do something.

It is not just simply a matter of asking a question, either: even when women use statements that would be, if transcribed, punctuated with a question mark, men can find ways to interpret them that are decidedly vague. 'Do you think you could take the rubbish out?' is, to me and most other women, quite clearly a direction, isn't it? Of course it is. But all but the most well-trained men think that this kind of question gives them the option of saying, 'Meh, no, I don't think I can. I can't be bothered, you see, I'm too busy organising my fantasy football team/playing with the dog/imagining how hot you would look in a nurse's uniform.' (Very hot, but that's not the point.)

What to take away from this? When it comes to questions, ladies, let's all attempt to prune our sentences and make our queries direct if we're addressing them to men. This isn't about being condescending or patronising; it's about being clear.

Gentlemen, don't ignore the possibility that what seems to you to be a simple observational statement from a woman may well, in fact, be a direct query that requires you to use up a substantial chunk of your daily word quota in order to formulate an adequate response. It may seem a costly use of your small budget of daily words, which you would prefer to apply in other situations, but take my (many) word(s) for it: it will pay off in the long run.

Tonality

Few women would disagree with the assertion that men show less emotion than we do when they speak, due to the massive social pressures for them to not talk about their feelings, much less shed a tear over anything other than their favourite sports team's attainment of some kind of league cup.

But British evolutionary biologists have recently proven that it's not just a matter of how both men and women describe their feelings: the tone of voice we use matters, too. Here's what they've discovered: while men (and Germans) are more often inclined to speak in an unemotional monotone, women are inclined to vary their tone in order to convey the emotion of a given statement. Thus, when we are in the midst of making our beloved tangential statements that are actually questions, it actually means something quite different from what the superficial meaning of that particular (excessively long) combination of words is . . . well, a man who pays attention to the pitch of a lady's voice may have a better chance at figuring out exactly what she is able to communicate through taking note of the variance in tones. Particularly if they are shrill, shrieky tones – in which case, I advise you, the woman in question may well be a bit displeased.

Women, on the other hand, must learn to discern the rather more subtle changes in men's tones of voice – and not to assume that an apparent monotone necessarily denotes a shocking lack of emotion, so much as it indicates that you could do with some kind of very sensitive ear trumpet. In other words, girls, dial down your iPod volume if you want to avoid loss of the kind of delicate hearing that might permit you to actually understand your boyfriend.

And get this – another thing that you can learn from the tone of a woman's voice is whether she is ovulating. Crazy, eh? Very recent research has apparently demonstrated that women's voices change in tone when we are at the most, ah, fruitful stage of our menstrual cycles, thus drawing men into our webs of fertility with throaty, Eartha Kitt purrs. Keep that in mind, gentlemen, next time you're listening to a husky-voiced lady narrating an advertisement for luxury ice cream. Your sudden desire for some sweet cold creaminess may, in fact, simply be a sublimated urge to impregnate her.

What? You're skipping dessert? But darling, it's *so delicious.*

Disclosing and eliciting personal information

Get this: Jonathan and Alice are at a party. Jonathan is in the living room chatting with their friend Maisie's new boyfriend, Toby; Alice is in the kitchen, telling Maisie how difficult she is finding life since Jonathan came back from his six-month secondment in America and started hanging his washing to dry all over their flat and spilling shower gel in the bathtub without cleaning it up ('It's soap. Soap is clean,' says Jonathan, in his nice manly literal fashion). Then Jonathan comes into the kitchen to find another drink.

'Well,' says Alice, with a note of approval in her voice, 'you and Toby are having great chats, aren't you?'

'Sure,' says Jonathan, pulling a can of lager from the fridge and popping it open.

'What are you talking about?' says Alice.

'Guess what we're talking about,' says Jonathan, taking a swig of his beer.

'Well,' says Alice, furrowing her delicate brow. 'Where you live? What you do for a living? Where you grew up? How you met your girlfriends?'

Jonathan smirks and shakes his head.

(Care to guess, readers?)

'Football,' Jonathan says.

Well, *obviously*.

When women make each other's acquaintance for the first time, we often follow a strict code of etiquette that involves quickly and silently assessing each other's appearance ('Is she prettier than me?' we can't help but wonder) followed by a rapid exchange of questions eliciting personal information of the sort that Alice had naïvely assumed that Jonathan would have exchanged with Toby. Men might find these questions to be overly probing – even rude – but women regard it not to be the third degree. Rather, we see it as simply a reasonable way of breaking the ice with a stranger and of getting to know someone – and, in the case of those of us who are rather competitive, comparing ourselves to her with the object of deciding whether or not we are more excellent.

Furthermore, a woman on the receiving end of this kind of mild line of interrogation usually chooses to regard another woman's queries about her personal life to be a sign of genuine interest, rather than simply a way to fill dead air in a conversation – even though she is quite aware, from her own use of the technique, that it might well be. I know that I'm not alone in being guilty of asking someone to tell me about his or her kids/job/shopping habits in order to allay my boredom with the other things he or she has to talk about (or lack thereof). But despite being perfectly well aware of that, I can't help but still feel quite excited when someone asks me to tell her about myself.

But this does not come as naturally to men. This is why it is important to keep in mind that when you are finding a chap to be somewhat opaque when it comes to divulging details of his personal life and innermost thoughts and feelings, it might not be that he is being intentionally obstructive. Rather, it might just not have occurred to him that you would find this information interesting, since he actually wouldn't necessarily be instantly fascinated if you started divulging the kind of mundane information about your life that you enjoy discussing with your girlfriends.

The solution? In these situations, I find it is useful to get the man in question chatting about his favourite football team/writer/political party – something less personal, in essence. Then, I patiently wait for him to be drawn on more fascinating aspects of his deepest thoughts and feelings –

after he's made my acquaintance for a few hours or months or years, he'll no doubt be more inclined to share. Patience can be required, however, which is why unless I really like a man, sometimes I find that it's just more entertaining to go and find another woman to talk to.

Technology

I am sure that you will have seen BBC costume dramas or films starring Daniel Day-Lewis at one time or another, so you will be aware that the strict rules of social etiquette once solved the problem of gender-influenced communication differences, through dictating that men and women should be prevented from communicating with each other as much as possible.

For example, after dinner in British upper-class homes, the men got to sit around the table smoking cigars and saying very few things while their wives were sent off to chit chat amongst themselves about girly issues like the state of their scullery maids and the best place to get corsetry done. (Both options sound terribly dull.) Sometimes, they got to do some stiff dancing in parallel lines of hot, simmering sexual tension. In less well-off families, I have learned from period television productions, men would tramp off to the pub after a long day down the mines or in the fields or wherever, while the women in their lives would pursue group activities like knitting, quilting and preserving things in jars. I would have found this style of womanhood to be slightly more fun, I think: I do like a spot of knitting and pickling, although I would have been quite resentful of the limited access to pints.

Certain contemporary circumstances do still promote this kind of gender-segregated discourse. Women consider getting manicures a group activity because one can sit there for a long time and have extraordinary conversations given an extra piquancy by the effects of the acetone fumes; men at the gym avoid chatting at all costs while lifting weights and secretly analysing whether they are sweating more or less than their buddies. But the degree to which the pressure is now on all of us to communicate with members of the opposite sex is not only truly unprecedented but also constant, thanks to a little phenomenon which you may have heard of: information technology.

And thus, as the noughties decade draws to a close, it is not just enough for all of us to attempt to communicate with the opposite sex with increasing frequency and frankness. Due to the ever-expanding number of modes of communication technology at our disposal, we now have to be prepared to communicate with them *all of the time*. Hilarity and awkwardness ensues. Let me take you through two crucial case studies, both of which have great significance with regards to inter-gender communication: text messaging and email.

Text messaging

With the advent of text messaging in the late nineties, men and women gained a particularly exciting new way to communicate with each other – or, rather, to mis-communicate with each other.

For men, the general social acceptance of texting as a legitimate way in which to communicate was like a big sparkly gift from a magical deity: finally, a mode of conversation in which saying as little as possible (or, you know, as I am sure that men no doubt prefer to think of it, 'being concise') is actually a tremendous advantage. Having been tyrannised for decades by the terrible pressure to take the initiative to actually make telephone calls to women in which they were expected to articulate whole sentences, men have collectively, albeit briefly, rejoiced over the technological development which has made it socially acceptable – even imperative – to express thoughts and feelings in a maximum of 144 characters. Indeed, many of them have even bravely accepted the challenge to do it in even fewer, unintentionally sending women such as myself who are on the receiving end of these truncated textual communications into spasms of confusion over what the meaning of 'oh-K' actually is. Does it mean 'OK'? Is it a bit sarcastic? Is it meant to be funny? Breathy? Why is there no punctuation? Oh, for heaven's sake!

On the other hand, character limits present women with an altogether different sort of challenge: how to reconcile our innate desire to communicate through the use of obtuse metaphors and delicate shades of meaning within the limitations of the short form of the SMS. For many women, writing text messages to men is a consummately difficult challenge. You might as well ask us to compose sonnets or Ph.D. dissertations. That's why we often take the team approach, wherein any one text message should properly be credited to as many authors as the average paper in a major science journal.

I have actually lost count of the number of times that I've found myself sitting around with a group of girls as one attempts to tap out a message to a new romantic interest with the collective input of a support team of three or four people. Entire evenings have been used up with this as the central form of entertainment. Many men would not believe that actual hours can elapse during the process of:

a) deciding how long we should wait until a text message is sent in response to a two- or three-line remark from a man

b) drafting the text message
c) gaining approval for each draft from our carefully selected panel of text message editors, with redrafting and editing conducted as needed
d) actually sending the text message

It is a huge waste of time, of course. It is a waste of time in which we girls could be engaging in all sort of more life-affirming activities with our thumbs. But we carry on, even as we know deep in our hearts that the recipients of our strenuous texting efforts will read a message that says, 'See you next Tuesday x' and think, 'Ah, I will see her next Tuesday', instead of what we dearly want them to think, which is: 'Well, she must be very busy and important if she can't see me until next Tuesday, no doubt because of the distractions provided by her multitudes of other suitors with whom I am in competition, and I am pleased to note that she has signed with a kiss, indicating affection, but only one kiss, indicating that while she is keen on our relationship, she is not in fact so keen that she is willing to make a fool of herself through sending me a profligate number of text smooches. I probably should buy her flowers.'

Email

Here's a fun way to spice up your love life: try conducting your next relationship without ever communicating with the object of your affection via email. On second thought, never mind – that is simply not possible. So impossible, indeed, that sometimes I feel a little bit of longing for the days when you had to telephone people, and thus communicate in a spontaneous and occasionally emotional fashion – now, communication that is not pre-meditated is so uncommon that when we do receive actual telephone calls, if there is the slightest bit of frisson between us and person on the line, we are most inclined to become slightly alarmed and hit 'reject' on our mobiles.

Speaking on the phone has become so rare that I didn't think it was completely strange that one man who I dated for six months emailed and texted me daily but never once telephoned me. Well, not until he phoned to tell me that he was breaking up with me because he was still in love with his ex-girlfriend. I knew something was terribly wrong as soon as my mobile screen informed me that he was calling, not texting. I rejected it, naturally, and rang him back later when I was feeling composed enough for the dropping of a relationship A-bomb.

As with email, the conflict between male brevity and the female tendency to hold forth at length again crops up in a most pressing fashion. While men may use email as a vehicle to convey functional messages with actual information in them, women tend to infuse our electronic epistles with heavy amounts of meaning inserted between the lines. And unlike in the case of text messages, email has no limitations as to what percentage of our daily word output can be applied to the communication. Result? We tend to, erm, go on a bit.

To: Jonathan Himglish
From: Alice Femalese
Subject: ce soir

Hello, Jonathan, how is your work day going? Mine is fine, although my boss has been particularly foul this afternoon, I suspect as a result of too many gin and tonics at lunch.
[Himglish translation: tell me a hilarious anecdote to amuse me, I'm bored.]
I just wanted to drop you an email to see what you are thinking

about our plans for the evening. [Himglish translation: Because I haven't heard from you, I have been driven to contact you even though my girlfriends have all told me that I should wait for you to take the initiative.]

Are you still interested in checking out that play that we were talking about on Saturday?

[Himglish translation: I am fearing that your silence is an indication of indifference.]

Perhaps one of us should look into arranging the tickets ahead of time in case they are sold out at the box office.

[Himglish translation: can you sort out the tickets, please? If I didn't want you to I would already have done it myself.]

If not, let me know if you have something else in mind . . . perhaps dinner somewhere?

[Himglish translation: Unless you have a very good excuse, I am expecting you to stick to our plans to see each other tonight.]

Alice x

To: Alice Femalese
From: Jonathan Himglish
Subject: re: ce soir

Sure! Let me know when.
[Femalese interpretation: I AM RELENTLESSLY MYSTERIOUS.]
xJ

Email also hugely facilitates the female need to communicate collaboratively – it's hard not to giggle when I run across a man who still thinks that he can send a woman a slightly controversial e-missive that is not then whipped round all of her friends within a few minutes. Not to mention that any responses men receive to their correspondence are reviewed by numerous women, taken through several drafts with changes dutifully tracked by the members of the same trusted editorial board that oversees text-messaging.

And thus, alas, in the case of emailing, both men and women again find ourselves in the throes of performing taxing mental exercises because we don't communicate like the opposite sex. Women assume that emails from men are full of hidden meaning; men think that emails from women should be taken at face value. Everyone is confused and sometimes embarrassed when their correspondence gets sent back to them, through a chain of hundreds of people, with cutting comments about how hilariously off-the-mark it is.

There is also a particular and rather peculiar immediacy issue with email. It's hard to dodge people's phone calls: they know you have a mobile, they know you carry it with you and they know you are not in a cave with no reception. When your call goes to voicemail after a couple of rings you know full well that the person you're trying to reach has bounced you because they're not interested in chatting. With email, however, we are still permitted to maintain a fiction that we do not have mobile Internet access at all times; on occasion, we even feel that it is OK to pretend that we haven't received an email, as if it can get lost like tangible post. 'Oh,' we say, 'I don't think I ever got that. Perhaps it got filtered into my junk mail folder. [By me, when I saw it and didn't want to read it.]' It would be very nice if we could all agree, right now, to abandon this silly pretense, but we don't, and we go on excusing other people making these kinds of preposterous claims, because we all want to have the loophole to fall back on in moments of utter communicative dysfunction.

Women, in particular, are inclined to exploit this to excess: many men don't realise that if they do not receive a swift response to their electronic correspondence, they can be quite sure that it is not because the lady has not read said correspondence but because she feels (or, perhaps her crack team of editorial consultants feels) that it is essential that she not be too hasty in her response. It's not that she's being rude, exactly, she's just trying to not seem needy, and as a result she is patiently counting down the minutes (or hours, or days) before she feels that her reply, composed almost immediately upon receipt of a missive, will be non-commital and utterly dignified.

On the contrary, my dear girls, when you think that a man is not responding to your email because he is trying not to seem needy, to let you dangle, he probably isn't. By now you'll be realising that blokes just don't think these things through nearly as much as we do. The time lapse is, I'm sorry to say, likely because he has a reason for not wanting to write back. At best, his delay is due to a reluctance to hurt your feelings or perhaps a terrible mishap (and no one wants to be in a situation where the best case scenario involves a terrible mishap); at worst, the delay is driven by indifference. That stings.

In summary . . .

What have we learned from this chapter? Here are some handy summaries, and I will offer you two more at the end of every chapter: pick your favourite.

Himglish: Men and women communicate differently. Sometimes, thinking about that will help you to understand women better.

Femalese: Women and men employ contrasting tactics in the realms of verbal and written communication,

sometimes prompting a certain degree of misunderstanding, as the result of differences in the
portent of signs, signifiers, and communicative
acts. This can potentially interfere with the
development or maintenance of mixed-gender
relationships. Consideration of the multiple
facets of discrepancies in modes of linguistic or
non-linguistic expression that may be predicated
by genetic or socialised gender differences has
the potential to alleviate misunderstandings and
promote an improved level of communication
with members of the opposite sex.

Do you understand? Of course you do. I'm quite proud of
you.

2

Dating: Let's Get Together. Whatever That Means

Anyone who has ever experienced adolescence – so, yes, that would be everyone – doesn't need to be told that his or her attraction to the opposite sex (or the same sex, for that matter) is a mysterious and often illogical phenomenon. One minute, you're happily knocking about in your tracksuit bottoms and playing computer games with your mates, dangling from monkey bars and sharing tea parties with your Barbie dolls. And the next minute, often with little warning of what new kind of chaos is about to be wrought on your life, you find that you are unnecessarily, often irritatingly, but inevitably and intractably preoccupied with the other half of the population, possibly to the detriment of your concentration in school and also, alas, your concentration for pretty much the rest of your life.

For what you don't realise when you are thirteen and experiencing the vagaries of love and attraction for the first time is that it doesn't really ever get any easier: we just get slightly better at coping with it. For men and women alike, the quest for romance is at once wonderful and difficult. It is often exhilarating, but it is also confusing and unfathomable and draining. And sometimes it can feel more than a little life-ruining.

But the most mysterious thing of all, I believe, is something that even the most plucky and bright evolutionary biologists may never quite be able to put their fingers on, no matter how many brains they scan. Despite the fact that the struggle to find someone to love is so universal, so essential, we are also universally (and essentially) embarrassed by the prospect of expressing our affection to someone of whom we are newly enamoured. Aren't we? And it sometimes seems like we are even less capable of turning that nascent love into something that might be described as a functional or, good heavens, enduring relationship.

Men and women undoubtedly often go about the process of searching for partners in remarkably different ways that are – though it seems a bit counterintuitive – not always complementary. But there are also some things we all have in common when it comes to the process of seeking partners. For example, starting from that fateful pubescent day when you adhered pictures of Keanu Reeves torn from magazines and newspapers to the ceiling above your bed with chewing gum (OK, maybe that was just me), regardless of your gender, you have probably devoted more of your life to unrequited admiration of longed-for romantic partners than to the actual romancing. Or, say, to learning useful, practical skills: just think how good you could be at something like welding or cake decorating if only you redirected a small fraction of the time you've spent having impossible crushes to learning new things. You could be amazing at them. And yet, you most likely aren't.

(I can't weld or cake decorate either, if that's any comfort.)

And a belief that the process of finding a partner can be achieved through adherence to some kind of rulebook is also one that crosses the gender divide – as does the belief that this rulebook is indistinct and more perplexing than the one you once had that purported to explain calculus. But are we making it harder for ourselves than is strictly necessary?

As you will have worked out already, my enthusiastic support for gender equality is boundless. But in the long march towards gender equality (we've not reached it yet, I think it is important to note) we have also had to accept that some areas of our lives have become a bit trickier as a result of our not being able to employ stereotypes with quite the aplomb that our ancestors did. And in particular, it is clear that the feminist movement has made the murky process of finding a partner significantly more challenging that it was in days of yore when men were men, women were women, the former always paid for dinner and the latter was in charge of being fragrant and of (ostensibly, at least) preventing any sexual intercourse from being had before wedding vows were said.

Now, please don't think for a second that I am advocating a return to patterns of behaviour that are musty and old-fashioned, because I am certainly grateful for the achievements of the feminist movement. In fact, despite the associated perils and wrenching of heartstrings, I think that dating (or courting, or hanging out or whatever the kids are calling it these days) is probably a lot more fun now than it was for our grandparents and even our parents, who were bound either by strict propriety or the intimidating burden of being the first generation to crash through those binds. But why, despite this apparent increase in fun, does the modern courtship remain something that is widely regarded as oh-so-difficult and generally complicated, and the source of a very great deal of bad feeling, and inspiration for the binge consumption of high-fat dairy products? In this chapter, let's try and figure out how, and why, and what it means, when we get together in the twenty-first century.

How you doing? Well, maybe not you.

Above all, the rather wild and disorganised approach that many of us take to dating is a symptom of not just an increasingly liberal society, but one in which our tremendous love of shopping means that we rarely acquire anything without being confronted with a vast array of choices. When making important (or even unimportant) decisions about what we want to buy, we have grown used to almost always being able to select from an enormous range of products that can be closely tailored to our personal preferences. Perhaps because of this range of choice, total satisfaction remains somewhat elusive. It is often impossible to suspend our awareness that even when we settle on something, we'll never be absolutely sure that it was the right decision, unless we have had the opportunity to sample a full range of alternatives. And thus, burdened by the anxiety that we might suffer buyer's remorse, the fear of making a decision can be crippling.

As with most consumer choices, finding someone to love, *really* love, is at heart a trial-and-error process. And that is why it is often best not to marry the first person you ever fancy. It is a process not unlike deciding what to eat for lunch. You can wander into a deli and pick the precise combination of garlic mayonnaise and herbed ciabatta and organic free-range chicken and Emmenthal made from perfectly delighted cows that you believe will be most delicious, but even as you take that first tasty bite, you may be distracted by the knowledge that you will never be sure what it would have been like with a little pesto and sun-dried tomatoes, on a bagel. And do you really need all of those carbs? Maybe you should be a vegetarian. And, of course, you don't make that decision in a vacuum: in many cases, your choice of sandwich will be strongly influenced by your past sandwich experiences. Maybe you think you love roast beef, so you ask for it even in vegetarian sandwich shops and are therefore always a bit disappointed, or perhaps mustard once gave you indigestion, which means that you will attempt to avoid it at all costs.

Some people might argue that those of you who are seeking a partner who you find physically attractive and interesting, and who makes good conversation and who enjoys the same kind of music that you do, and who holds sympathetic views to yours with regards to how much it is acceptable to talk during films and the superiority of butter over margarine and the merits of the work of the post-modern novelist Don DeLillo, are being picky to an unacceptable extent. But while the criteria that some people use for vetting potential partners may seem a bit eccentric, we have always employed strange and distinct and frankly unromantic methods to figuring out who to fall in love with, whether it was based on common religious beliefs or guaranteed financial security or regular sex with someone who is also kind enough to look after the upkeep of your home, bear your children, and darn your socks. Being selective in these circumstances is nothing to be ashamed of, but neither is having those lonely moments when you think it would just be nice to have a partner – any partner. (I most often feel that way when I am at the shops restocking pantry staples and realise that I can't buy the cheaper-by-volume enormous bottle of olive oil because I don't have a willing partner to help me to carry it home.)

Of course, I have come to this conclusion in part because I am quite selective myself: in my callow youth, I actually wrote down a list of twenty-eight things that I required in a putative boyfriend, including 'must like dogs', 'must not be a picky eater' and 'does not spend more time grooming his hair than I do mine'. Although with maturity I have realised that there is something to be said for a certain degree of flexibility, the temptation to refer to my list remains strong. Except that with the wisdom of years I have learned that sometimes it is completely OK to suspend one's prejudices for a really special person, and then I feel utterly generous and broad-minded on the rare occasions that I deign to step out with vegan cat-fanciers who sport pompadours.

And, of course, though I personally enjoy my boyfriend rubric, it is important for all of us to note that no matter how many lists we make, our dedicated searches for perfect partners are frequently and hopelessly derailed by the ineffable magic of romantic attraction, thanks to our primeval instincts and complicated genetic programmes. You may be surprised to find out the strange things that our DNA dictates when it comes to dating: for example, that women will be attracted to men who look like our fathers. (Much to my delight, this ancient rumour was confirmed by a late-2007 study, which vindicated me for the time that I went out with a man who bore such an unnerving resemblance to my father that I phoned up Dadelstein and demanded a detailed alibi for his whereabouts nine months before the dad-alike's birth.) And it is also a fact that is proven by science that men will often be drawn to women with symmetrical features because it is an indicator that they will produce healthier babies, even if the symmetry-fancying men have no conscious urge to reproduce – or, indeed, perish the very thought.

And furthermore (furthermore!), single life will be a lot less disappointing once more of us accept that not finding anyone who is just right no matter how hard you try is more of a possibility than it ever was before, especially now that the state of being a singleton is far from uncommon. In the UK, the number of people who have never married anyone and who live alone and who are, despite these apparent handicaps, not necessarily pathetic, is higher than ever before, with single men outnumbering single women substantially. Indeed, it is almost widely accepted that men can learn to wield feather dusters themselves rather than get married simply to ensure that their homes will be kept tidy. And, I think we can also extrapolate from that statistic, it is only a little less widely acknowledged that women can be quite happy having these nifty things called careers and may not want to commit themselves to a few pre-divorce years of being weighed down by an inappropriate husband just so they don't ruin the gender balance at formal dinner parties. (Of course, hardly anyone is having formal dinner parties anymore. Which, unlike all the other fusty traditions mentioned here that I am glad to have seen fade away into obscurity, is a shame. Bring back formal dinner parties, I say, without bringing back rampant sexism.)

In summary? Many of us have now wholeheartedly embraced the belief that we should look for a partner of the opposite sex who we actually like, rather than merely someone with the inversion of our own genitalia.

Hello, Hercules? Here is your task. By comparison, cleaning horse manure out of the world's biggest barn is cake.

Dating online is not just for geeks. It's just not for admitting.

Alice was minding her own business, that rainy Sunday afternoon in late March, taking the bus into the centre of town to meet her friend Eleanor for tea. Alice wasn't a habitual taker of buses, but she was running late and it was bucketing down, so she squeezed on to the crowded vehicle with a host of other grumpy, rain-sodden, Sunday-afternoon travellers.

One of whom, she was shortly to realise, would change her life for ever.

Was it the fateful rain that did it, by forcing them on to the bus to travel a short distance that both of them would usually just walk? Or was it that a squirrel was sent by fate to run in the path of the bus? Or, perhaps, was the hand of destiny involved in the fact that the bus driver was a committed vegetarian who couldn't bear the possibility of taking the life of an innocent squirrel? In any case, the driver braked suddenly, sending the passenger next to Alice hurtling into her.

'I'm so sorry,' he said, removing himself from her personal space.

'It's all right,' Alice said, looking up at her unwitting assailant.

Jonathan smiled down at her. She smiled back.

'I think this could be the beginning of a beautiful friendship,' said Jonathan. And it was.

Or it would have been, if it had actually happened. But that's just a rather sweet story that Alice made up for her and Jonathan to tell people who ask them how they met, because somehow the truth seems too shameful: actually, Alice and Jonathan met on the Internet.

Remember when Internet dating was strictly for geeks, a world of romance specifically designed for people who spoke programming languages more fluently than they understood their native tongues and preferred contact with their keyboards to making eye contact? It wasn't so very long ago at all, really. But a handful of years is a very long time in technological terms and, like Jonathan and Alice, although we may not have the confidence to admit to it in public, an awful lot of us – hundreds of thousands of us – are trawling the World Wide Web for love.

With the current generation of twenty- and thirty-somethings having come of age in tandem with digital technology, it makes perfect sense that we employ it to find romance, just as our ancestors engaged in very specific social rituals in the course of finding life partners. Having read a number of sociological studies on courtship conventions in, for example, turn-of-the-twentieth-century provincial France (yes, I do these things so you don't have to) I've concluded that we use the Internet in a contemporary version of a ritualised search for love not unlike the tea dance or the debutante ball or the awkward coincidental encounter that was once arranged by a well-meaning grandmother who felt that time was running out and it was high time that you got hitched to her very nice and high-earning, if uncharismatic, oral surgeon, or her friend Mabel's pretty, if dim, granddaughter.

While many argue that it is still for geeks, finding a partner online has become such a mainstream activity that one recent American study performed by a pollster who, in advance of the 2008 presidential election, was trying to understand just what made his countrymen tick, found that almost ten per cent of American newly-weds met their partners online, leading to their designation as a whole special demographic of people known as 'Internet marrieds'. What unites this demographic besides the way that they met is still not entirely clear – they invite their laptops to the wedding? They can type quite rapidly? – but I think it means, in any case, that finding a partner through the magic of hypertext mark-up language is no longer embarrassing.

Or, at least, slightly less embarrassing than it once was,

particularly because if you feel so inclined, you and your Internet beloved can, like Jonathan and Alice, concoct a perfectly adorable fiction of how you met each other that will bring tears to the eyes of even the most hard-hearted listener and make far better material for a wedding speech than 'I clicked on his profile by mistake and was immediately swept away by the dual revelations that he preferred the same brand of baked beans to me and lived in a convenient neighbourhood that could be easily accessed by public transport'.

Anyway, having given it a shot myself (purely for research purposes, of course), my verdict is that there are many things that make dating via the Internet great, not least of which is that it offers you the opportunity to shop for a partner as if you are flicking through a catalogue looking for a pair of new shoes. Unlike merely hooking up with someone cute who you clap eyes on in the pub (or who falls on top of you on the bus), before you even meet you have the opportunity to establish that you have something in common, that you might actually have something to talk about, and that you will be unlikely to have a huge disagreement for at least the first ten minutes of your encounter (unless, of course, one of you has been lying on your profile).

Unfortunately, as is the case all too often when you try to buy shoes from a catalogue, many a time a pair that looks fetching when you select them may well turn out to be ill-fitting or poorly manufactured or wrong with the rest of your outfit – things that you would have been able to discern quite easily if you had gotten off your sofa and gone to the shop in person in order to give the merchandise at least a cursory glance. It's terribly easy for people to misrepresent themselves online, and it's even easier for online shoppers, so to speak, to make assumptions and project hopes upon what or who they are ordering up because they badly want the shoes/potential partner to be a perfect fit.

Women, in particular, are in danger of this kind of disappointment: with our proven penchant for romantic narrative, in contrast to the male penchant for visual stimulation, as a route to weak knees, it can be all too easy to make the jump from being the recipient of some witty email banter to drawing the conclusion that we have – at last! – found the sure-to-be father of our future children, which only makes it all the more disappointing when he turns up to meet you for that first introductory drink and is completely unfanciable or offensive or boring. Or, worse yet, for the gentleman you have been dreaming of to think one of those things about you.

While they may be less inclined to start scripting romance novels starring themselves and the girl at the other end of the email, men are inclined to suffer their own online-dating anxieties: with their relatively compromised tendency to understand the delicate shades of meaning that women inject into their own writing and attempt to eke from what they read – for more on this, do refer back to the chapter on communication – chaps can find themselves rocking up for an innocent drink, little knowing that they have inadvertently indicated to the lady that their intentions are more than casual. Awkward.

To google or not to google?

Even if you would never dream of going on a date with someone you met on the Internet, that doesn't mean that the World Wide Web is not going to play a role in your romantic life in one way or another, unless you are a diehard Luddite. I suppose back in olden times when you were going to go out with someone new you might ask mutual acquaintances to share information about them. If there were no mutual acquaintances, you were plum out of luck. Nowadays, there are very few people who are Google-immune: all it takes is a few keystrokes and you will be privy to all sorts of random pieces of information about the person you're meeting up with tomorrow night for drinks. In my own experience (and through surveying my friends), it's apparent that women are much more compulsive about googling their dates than men, perhaps because, as I mentioned above, in comparison to men, we tend to be initially attracted to someone on the basis of our impression of his personality rather than his physique.

Thanks to social networking sites like Facebook – not to mention the profusion of people who choose to share the minutiae of their daily lives through blogging – stalking, or as I like to call it, researching, someone before you get to know them properly has never been easier. It's a strange and not always useful undertaking, however, because it doesn't really do anything to allay the stress of a first date – and, in many cases, makes it worse. Unlike with Internet dating, where you have mutually, explicitly shared information, covert Facebook-stalking means that you are not (according to the rules of propriety) allowed to reveal that you already know that your new love interest is passionate about long-distance cycling and had a nose job. Thus you are compelled to feign fascination and surprise when the cycling and nose job are revealed to you in the course of conversation.

Now, I did once go out with one young man who contacted me after reading my blog and who, perhaps because that was how we met in the first place, wasn't ashamed to admit that he'd done a little bit of Internet stalking. 'We've googled each other,' he remarked, with utmost ease, five minutes after we met in person, and then we both laughed and were able to move the conversation forward without having to pretend to be starting from the absolute beginning. However, few people are so bold since even though we all do it, searching for people on the Internet has not yet crossed the fine line that divides that which is creepy and that which is socially acceptable. It may never be OK. On another occasion, for example, a man I'd seen once before greeted me on our second encounter with the exciting news that he had downloaded a photo of me from the Internet to his phone. Bursting with pride, he thrust the screen into my line of vision for me to admire. 'That's, uh, nice,' I said, frantic to think of a convincing fake emergency that would justify the fleeing that I was about to do.

I suppose that the most romantic option is to abstain from researching someone beforehand if you really like him, to give him a chance to prove himself to you in person rather than through a series of compromising photos that an unkind friend has posted on Facebook. Even if the information that you find is appealing, there is also a danger that your imagination can run away with you. The more you string the clues together in your head before actually getting to know someone, the more you run the risk of being disappointed simply because he or she will surely fail to match up to the perfect specimen you've imagined.

But, of course, resisting the opportunity to avail yourself of the information that is out there for public consumption is also not the most efficient option, since without doing that online background check, it might take rather longer in the course of your budding relationship to discover that the man you are dating has served time in prison for stealing money from his grandmother, or the woman you're falling for is already married to someone else. And by then you might be dangerously in love. I suppose it all rather depends on how much of a hopeless romantic you are, and the degree to which you are willing to throw caution to the wind when it comes to matters of the heart. But since we are now so used to having information at our fingertips about absolutely everything else, it is not surprising that we are not as eager to crash blindly into romance as we were before the advent of digital broadband.

Shall we split the bill? And other love-extinguishing moments.

Alice and Jonathan are in a restaurant on their first date. It is going well: they gaze lovingly into each other's eyes. The waitress places the bill on the table.

Jonathan: Ah, the bill has arrived.
[Femalese intepretation: I should probably pay for this but in today's progressive era of gender equality, do I really have to?]
Alice: How much do I owe you? Now, where did I put my wallet?'
[Himglish translation: Say 'nothing'! Say 'nothing'!]
Jonathan: £22.50.
[Femalese interpretation: I have totally missed the fact that your wallet grab was merely a ruse. I am not aware that if you really wanted to pay, you would have physically picked up the bill your-self to examine the details. I'm either kind of an idiot, or simply some kind of pedant who feels compelled to call your bluff.]
Alice: Oh, that's fine then.
[Himglish translation: You're kind of an idiot. Or maybe a bluff-calling pedant. I will let you get away with it because I still find you kind of adorable, but I am going to go home and tell all my friends about this and then, oh! How we shall laugh at your expense.]

OK, so you've picked someone lovely from the catalogue (or from the crowd at the bar, or your best friend has set you up with a guy she knows from work, or a handsome specimen has fallen off his bicycle in front of you). You've googled him or looked through all of his photographs on Facebook and assessed your level of relative attractiveness in comparison to his ex-girlfriend (hint: your dating experiences will be much more successful if you keep in mind that you are always inherently more attractive than the ex-girlfriend in one way or another, because you haven't broken up with him yet). Now, of course, things only become more treacherous, for you must actually socialise with this potential object of your affection. In person. In public.

Even establishing that you are on a date in the current social climate can be a bit tricky, since it is just as common and acceptable for men and women to go out in platonic pairs as in romantic ones. This is, of course, a totally great progression in social conventions that expands our opportunities for rich friendships with the opposite sex. But it also results in what I like to call the *ambigudate*, wherein you find yourself on an outing with a member of the opposite sex but can't quite tell what the purpose of the outing is, thus putting you in a position where you must attempt to decode vague clues about your companion's intentions – is he buying you a lot of drinks? Is she wearing a new outfit? In many cases, you will remain unable to gauge what is going on unless the encounter ends in a passionate clinch or a fraternal cheek-peck.

Perhaps even more awkward than the ambigudate is the *accidate*, when a man and a woman go out together motivated by completely different assumptions. Most often, an accidate occurs when the gentleman thinks that it's a date and the lady thinks that it is merely a friendly outing. This is because many very well-meaning men (in my experience, it is particularly common with those who have spent a lot of time in all-male educational institutions) have a rather sweet but slightly tragic tendency to extrapolate that an attractive woman who makes eye contact with them must be interested in romancing them, when in fact the lady in question is just being quite friendly. Women, in contrast, tend to be a little bit more adept at differentiating between chemistry and *chemistry*, although we too make mistakes from time to time and find ourselves the instigators of accidates.

Accidates don't end well, and they usually end with embarrassment – if you're lucky, the person who has accidentally gone on a date with you will namedrop her boyfriend or mention that he prefers to go out with men before you do something silly and make an unwarranted pass. But oftentimes people are not lucky, which is why I would consider the merits of at least trying to communicate the nature of your interest in a slightly less-than-subtle way before the outing itself. Sure, telling someone you fancy him or her can be embarrassing and difficult, but it's less embarrassing than having that person squeal and push you away when you think you are about to have a special moment and they think you are leaning in to remove a stray eyelash from their cheek. This is always going to be more damaging to your confidence in the long-term than if you suggest a date to someone and he says that he would love to if he wasn't married or more interested in dating people of the same sex or committed to spending all of his evenings for the foreseeable future perfecting his wheatgerm muffin recipe, an activity which must be carried out in total isolation in order to ensure he is giving it his full attention.

But even if you have established that you are indeed on an actual date, figuring out how to operate is a new challenge unto itself. Many gentlemen would benefit from knowing this special, secret and enormously valuable tip: although they may well be very delighted to make more money than you/ask you out/kiss you first/defeat you at arm-wrestling, most women would prefer you to take the lead when you are taking them out for the first time. This is not because they are retrograde and anti-feminist or because they are cheap; it's because on the whole, no one wants to be in charge on a first date. Most men, you see, would also quite like the woman to take the lead when they are going out the first scary time. Result? No one takes any initiative, and what could have been The Greatest Love Of All can fizzle into The Greatest Near-Miss Of All Due to Mutual Reluctance to Take A Risk.

So, women tend to assert that it is the man's job because there is less historical precedent for the reverse. Being able to relinquish this particular responsibility to a man is one of the few aspects of 1950s womanhood that many otherwise modern and liberated women cling to, even if it makes us feel like we are letting down our feminist credentials. But many men don't buy that argument (maybe rightfully so) and don't take the initiative because they think that they are being modern and forward-thinking; unfortunately, this just makes women feel like these men are being lazy and a bit lame, doesn't it? I've never come across a woman who remarked of her new love interest, 'He lets me pay for things all the time, and it's great!' but I have more than once found myself discussing a new man in the life of one or other of my female friends, who has blown her socks off by actually calling her on the phone.

My grandmother adhered to the adage, 'Men should do the chasing.' And while my grandmother was born in 1907 and thus may have had *slightly* old-fashioned attitudes towards romance, the appreciation – and, to some extent, the expectation – of being chased really has stuck with me, and with a lot of other women.

Is this anti-feminist? Well, that is definitely debateable. Yes, it is maybe quite bizarre for many women to wish to be treated as equal to men in all situations with the exception of this one. But the fact remains that in an era of supreme ambiguity brought on by the trend that in many circles it is perfectly acceptable to sleep with someone on a regular basis and deny that he or she is anything more than a friend, picking up the bill is one of the simplest ways in which to signal your romantic intentions without declaring them outright.

What's the solution to this dilemma? Quite simply, that the person who issues an invitation should take responsibility for paying if he or she wishes to express romantic intentions. And this responsibility needs to be taken assertively: no one likes having to do the fake wallet grab, when the bill comes and you dive into your handbag or trouser pocket in the pretence that you're happy to split it.

No, we're just friends now, even though we used to have extremely hot sex.

Being a sociable type, I will rarely turn down the opportunity to go on a date with someone new – at worst, I reckon, I'll get a hilarious story out of it, and even if we don't fall in love I might make an interesting new friend. This was my thinking a few months again when I went out with a guy who I had met very briefly at a party. I really didn't know him at all well, but I went on a date with him for the usual reasons: he was kind of cute, he was friendly, he seemed to quite enjoy my company. We had a drink and chatted about our lives in that first-date-y kind of way. He told me about his job. He told me about his dog (excellent). And he told me about his divorce, which was a little surprising, since he was all of twenty-seven years old (not excellent). 'Oh,' I said, in my most sympathetic voice, 'that must have been difficult' as I wondered whether they had to return their wedding gifts or if he was still in possession of some really good kitchen equipment. 'It was,' he said, looking a little sad. But then he visibly brightened. 'I mean,' he explained, 'my ex-wife and I are still really close. And we still live together, since it's cheaper.'

That's nice, isn't it? Maybe it is really nice for him and his ex-wife. But it is not the kind of information that exactly makes a girl's heart sing on a first date, or really on any date. But these days, dealing with these kinds of complicated scenarios is nearly inevitable. Of all the interesting challenges you will be sure to run across in the twenty-first-century quest for romance, one of the most unique and endemic is the relatively recent habit that people have of hanging on to their former partners for years under the guise of friendship, even following truly bitter splits. Both men and women are guilty of doing this, and we're almost all guilty of allowing it to make us jealous.

That jealousy is expressed in many different ways. We tend to assume that women are always the more jealous party – this is, I believe, based on a retro belief that men aren't really meant to be faithful, so that when the women in their lives are unhappy about them rubbernecking other ladies in the street, it is a display of unnecessary harridanness. In contrast, of course, conservative views hold that women are necessarily the exclusive property of the man who they profess to love, so naturally those men should feel justified in getting all up in the grill of the chap who is checking out their girlfriend. As a result, women tend to – surprise! – be slightly more passive-aggressive when it comes to telling their boyfriends that they're not happy about relationships with (or ogling of) other women because of their desire not to be labelled as jealous biddies. Men, on the other hand, may be more forthright because expressions of jealousy can be construed to serve as markers of masculinity.

Jonathan: Great news! Elizabeth and Tony can come to our dinner party!

Alice: Oh, isn't that wonderful? So nice of you to take the initiative to invite her, because I always so enjoy spending time with your ex-girlfriend, much as I also find a way to derive a twisted pleasure from going to the dentist.

[Himglish translation: You have got to be kidding me.]

Jonathan: Did you see the way that guy looked at you? Maybe I should punch him.

[Femalese interpretation: Me Tarzan.]

Alice: Or maybe for efficiency's sake I should just break up with you now and cut out the part where you break your knuckles?

Up until quite recently, you were rarely expected to remain on friendly terms with anyone you had once dated, much less socialise on a regular basis with someone who you had once known in the Biblical sense. Rare, for example, that your mum introduces you to Fred, the guy she used to date before she cheated on him with your dad, or your dad invites Florence, his girlfriend from the sixth form, over to the family home for supper and a catch-up.

Yes, for that generation, once it was over, it was really over: your formerly beloved was dead to you. At best, if you ran into each other in the supermarket there might be some sort of exchange of cursory nods, but etiquette allowed for the possibility that you might just as easily choose to stare through the erstwhile object of your affection as if he or she wasn't there. Ducking into the cereal aisle and hiding behind an economy-sized packet of Shredded Wheat was also a perfectly legitimate option. You didn't have to pretend.

Go back a few more years, of course, and the norm was that adults were not really allowed to have friends of the opposite sex, regardless of whether they had ever been romantically involved, unless the opposite-sex friends were half of a couple that you and your partner hung out with (or unless you were some kind of raging counter-cultural pioneer). Several women of my mother's generation have shared with me how their otherwise quite reasonable husbands remain uncomfortable with the prospect of them having male friends, even thought the said male friends fit into the category that was once popularly known as confirmed bachelors, and is now popularly known as gay best friends.

But now this all seems really unacceptably dull. These stringent rules meant that in many cases, the two halves of a foundered relationship were permanently estranged, which meant that potentially beautiful friendships went unrealised or were rent asunder. It was very sad, and I think we should be very pleased that we have done away with this post-relationship rigidity: just because two lovely people aren't ultimately meant to love each other, one needn't assume that they can't still share an excellent friendship. It's a shame to see the two as mutually exclusive.

But as with so many other trends, we've now turned the norm so unequivocally upside down that our post-break-up behaviour often pushes things to the other extreme. Not only must you cope with the often deeply galling experience of maintaining civil and frequent discourse with someone with whom you shared hot, sweaty, naked times and told all your deepest darkest secrets to before he or she ripped your heart out of your chest and kicked it about like a football (can be rewarding, yes, but oh! it can also require a hell of a lot of teeth-gritting). But it is not uncommon for us to find ourselves pressed to engage in some form of friendship with the ex-partners of our current partners, and the current partners of our ex-partners. And much as this has the possibility to be utterly droll, more often than not it can also be the cause of a great deal of frowning (not good for the ageing skin, you know) and a wave of that particular kind of empty dread that social obligation strikes into your heart – usually experienced, if you are a woman, at that moment when you are stroking on your mascara in anticipation of the night out that you don't want.

And yet in our ever-valiant attempts to show how cool and liberal and free-willed we are, expressions of reluctance to spend time with your ex-partner or your partner's ex-partner or your partner's ex-partner who used to go out with your ex-partner (it happens) are considered to be terribly gauche. If you explain to your boyfriend that you'd rather not hang out with his ex-girlfriend from college who his parents loved and adored so much that they cried for days when she dumped him (but they really like you too, sure they do) then he is likely to accuse you of being unnecessarily jealous and a bit crazy (you're not). But at the same time, if you're a man who remarks to your girlfriend that you'd prefer to stay home with her tonight rather than attending her ex-boyfriend's thirtieth birthday party, you might as well tattoo 'control freak' across your forehead – backwards, naturally, so you can read it when you look in the mirror (don't). Which is a shame really. I think it would all be much easier if we could just admit that – yes! – jealousy in these kinds of scenarios is perfectly natural.

I am not ashamed to admit I am just as bad as the rest of you in weaving this kind of emotional tangled web. Like many women, I have kept in touch with several of my ex-boyfriends, and a couple of sub-boyfriends who I dated briefly before it became apparent that we really just should have ignored the possibility of romance and gone straight to a jolly platonic friendship – I liked them a lot, but not in that way. I dearly value all of these relationships in their current manifestations, and although I am generally sweetness personified, I would certainly feel that it was necessary to commence a small brouhaha if any future boyfriend of mine dared to suggest that I should have to cut off all contact with these chaps because my relationship with them was in some way inappropriate or ambiguous or threatening to him. But in spite of that, I am certain that I will always have to make a concentrated effort to hold back my natural instinct to feel a bit sulky every time a boyfriend of mine spends time with one of his equally platonic former female companions.

Some people ascribe this particular form of jealousy to a fear of infidelity, but in fact if you look deep inside your heart I think you already know that it's not that likely that you actually think that your boyfriend is meeting up with his ex-girlfriend in order to shag her, or that he is worrying that you are likely to flee to Bali with that bloke you used to go out with when you were thirteen, after you meet him at the school reunion and discover that he has passed five feet in height. Rather, I think that discomfort with your partner's former flames is due to a sort of fear of retroactive infidelity – no matter how whole and fulfilling and genuine your relationship is, you can never own the time that your partner spent with his exes when they were together.

And thus it sometimes is difficult not to feel a little bit begrudging of the fact that the person with whom you are tremendously happy also used to be tremendously happy with someone else with whom he had intimate emotional moments that you'll never know about. And thus you will never be unequivocally certain that the emotional intimacy (and physical intimacy, for that matter) that you've shared with him is better, because you weren't there. And you'll dislike that, even though you may well know perfectly well that you are one of those people against whom the grudge is held by the women your ex-boyfriends are now involved with. And you'll be reminded of that grudge every time you hear that person's name or find yourself somehow compelled to spend time with her.

What's the solution? The most obvious one, of course, is to only go out with people who have spent the last ten years doing scientific research on their own in frozen arctic climes and are thus unburdened by past lovers. This is, however, difficult to accomplish. The second most obvious solution is this: when confronted with this particular sticky wicket, I find the crucial thing is that we simply must just try to be kind. Yes, you will selfishly want to carry on seeing your ex, you will egotistically think that there is nothing wrong with maintaining a close friendship that you know is now perfectly *sans frisson*. But for the sake of goodness, do please consider, first and foremost, the feelings of your new partner.

Jealousy is rarely rational, but that doesn't mean that telling the person who is expressing jealousy that he or she is being irrational is a legitimate way to deal with the problem. And, alas, relationships do require sacrifices some- times, no matter how much in these spoiled times we seem to expect them not to. And if your former partner can't see that he should no longer be the first priority in your life, that your friendship just can't be as intense when there are new partners in the mix, then he is not being especially kind either.

And the inverse? If your partner is continuing to maintain what you believe to be an inappropriately close friendship with his ex, despite your obvious (by which I mean clearly communicated) discomfort and your effort to extend at least a superficial hand of friendship to that woman yourself? Maybe he's not actually kind enough for you to be in a relationship with.

Yes, I know it's all a bit difficult. Life is a bit difficult.

Is there even a point to this besides the free dinner?

It is a truth universally acknowledged that a single man in possession of good fortune, or one who is flirtatious despite his relative poverty, will be initially attracted to a woman purely on the basis of her physical characteristics. It is similarly acknowledged that a single woman will base her assessment of a potential suitor in the first instance on less superficial parameters, but not really: the personality traits that one can convey, in the first five minutes, after all, tend not to be exceedingly broad or necessarily reflective of one's genuine self, particularly if you spend three of the five minutes giggling because the girl who is talking to you is so cute.

When it comes to connecting with members of the opposite sex, rather than going to comportment classes (boys) or getting plastic surgery (girls), I think it is far better to look to the excellent advice of my grandfather, Arthur S. Edelstein, a man who, as he was sadly widowed twice, has had three marriages to excellent ladies over the course of his ninety-odd years, and is therefore quite an expert. 'Jean,' he intoned in his most solemn, sage-like tone after news of me being the recipient of a particularly galling 'It's not you, it's me, but it's really you' speech rippled through the family gossip channels, 'love is like baseball. You can get some strikes, as long as you get one hit.'

Thanks, Grandpa Edelstein! The fact of the matter is that most of us, with the exception of the minuscule few who cleave for life to their first girlfriend or boyfriend, date a lot of people over the years, most of whom will have something wrong with them (of course, this wrong thing may well be that they simply don't appreciate quite how toothsome you are).

Thus, rather than fretting too much about whether you have carefully tailored your appearance or attitude to appeal to the base desires of the opposite sex, I think that it is ultimately much better to view this romance lark with a sense of humour. That way, you always win: either you will fall in love and live happily ever after (or for three months, until he expresses his fear of commitment or she declares that she's having an affair with her boss . . . but it will be a fun three months) or you will have a hilarious story to tell at parties. And the circle of people paying rapt attention to your brilliant, witty anecdotes will make you seem very attractive to members of the opposite sex who haven't met you yet, but who themselves will soon be queuing up for the opportunity to be the next person to provide you with love, sex, and hilarious stories to tell at parties.

Yes, there is something else that I haven't mentioned.

Now, you are probably thinking, 'Jean, all of this is rather helpful and interesting, but you have barely scratched the surface of the most important and troublesome challenge that men and women must confront when it comes to romance: sex.

Don't fret! That's the entire next chapter.

In summary . . .

Himglish: Dating is fun but confusing. Be honest, flexible, and have a sense of humour when you're doing it. And take the initiative. But don't be offended if a woman does instead.

Femalese: The initial stages of finding a perfect partner can be viewed as a complex matrix of communication, emotion, and sexuality that is strongly influenced by social expectations and mores as well as the personal experiences of individuals. Clarifying expectations through clear conveyance of your feelings and desires, in addition to patience with potential partners, will help you to maximise the fun and success of the experience.

3

Sex: Everything You Thought You Knew About Sex is Wrong (Except the Bits Which Are Right)

I remember so clearly when I first found out that sex existed. My parents had never opted for one of those semi-magical explanations involving storks and cabbage patches: I knew that my mother had been pregnant, that I had rocked into the world in our local public hospital, but I had no idea of the details of what came before that stage. Until I was eight.

Yes, I was eight, a sweet and innocent eight, and I was round at my friend's house after school. She was, of course, my most exciting and edgy eight-year-old friend, and in the spirit of eight-year-old edginess she decided to show off to me the books that her parents had given her in order to avoid having to talk to her about the facts of life. It was a much bigger deal than when I found out that there wasn't a Santa Claus: I sat on the floor and flipped through the pages, agog. The contents of those slim volumes went well beyond my wildest eight-year-old imaginings. It is rather hilarious, I think, that I was convinced for several years after this incident that it was perfectly normal for teenage girls to get pregnant without getting undressed, because my friend and I were interrupted by her mother in our reveries just as I was reading the section warning about teen pregnancy, about how sometimes teenagers would 'caress each other through their clothes'. Presumably it went on to discuss how the clothes were then removed, leading to sexual intercourse, but it was a few more years before I actually found that out.

Following that fateful afternoon, I then spent the next two years pretending when in the presence of my parents that I hadn't a clue about sex, because I didn't want them to be upset about my shattered innocence. Most painful was the need to stifle laughter at the double entendres while we sat around on Saturday nights watching *Are You Being Served?*, until an impending course in Sex Ed at school meant that my mother at last decided that it was time for me to know the facts of life, after all. We walked around the neighbourhood and she told me that sometimes when a man and a woman love each other very much, they both take their clothes off and . . . I twisted my face into an expression that I hoped could be taken for one that conveyed astonishment.

And although that was the best part of two decades ago, and I am certain I am now allowed to know where babies come from, I must confess that I still find myself making that facial expression from time to time when sex comes up as a topic for discussion – which is often, of course. Because despite the fact that we are all bombarded daily with sex in the media, in our chats with friends – why, sometimes, even in our romantic relation-ships – I never cease to be amazed by the immense amount of brainpower and fretting that both men and women devote to the somewhat quixotic task of understanding the rules and ethics and nuances that are part and parcel of our sex lives and our collective attitudes towards sex and sexuality. It's almost as if we are still eight years old. I mean, yes, it is an absolutely fascinating topic, with a lot of space for interesting exploration (both literally and figuratively) but I also think we might all be a little less anxious if we were to accept that the human race has been having sex for so very long that if it really was entirely comprehensible, we likely would have figured it out already. Perhaps we would be a little happier in our sex lives if we all agreed to accept that we will always be a bit mystified by it.

Yes, lovely readers, it is now safe to assume that we are living in an era that has told us that all of our past assumptions about what sex means to men and women are completely wrong. Except for the cases in which they are absolutely correct. Are you confused yet? Of course you are.

In these heady early twenty-first-century years, it is quite possible that both men and women have never been so free to exercise sexual self-determination. And yet, perhaps because of all of this freedom, it can also seem that having an unprecedented range of sexual options available to us means that men and women have never, ever been so perplexed about sex. I think what we need to aim for is a compromise (I love compromises, of course): wouldn't we all be happier if we admitted that we sometimes can't help but operate according to what we perceive are the rules, but also that we are aware of how rarely these so-called rules really apply, how vastly inadequate they can be in terms of helping us to determine the course of our sex lives? We would be happier, we would!

Now, before we dive in, I think it is important to note that one of the most crucial points of departure for all of this confusion is, of course, what many people call 'the double standard' and what I call 'making unrealistic, inaccurate and dangerous assumptions about female sexuality'. The double standard is something that few of us were not indoctrinated with from a young age, partly by our parents, other adults, and our contemporaries, and partly because we learn about it through osmosis, even if we have been otherwise shielded, thanks to the media.

What do we know? Women have sex for love. Men will have sex with anything. Women should be in charge of saying 'no'. Men will always try to get women to say 'yes'. Sex early in a new relationship means that it is bound to fail. Women should do what they can to avoid having too many sexual partners. Men should try to collect as many partners as possible. Women use sex to coerce men into commitment. It is unnatural for men to commit to monogamous sexual relationships.

At least, we thought we knew all of that, until the advent of feminism. And, more recently, the advent of a 24/7 media landscape that is more saturated with sexual content than any we've ever previously experienced. We thought we knew all of that until the advent of *Sex and the City* and media of its ilk pushed consideration of female sexuality more centrally into mainstream conversation that it had ever been before, when we became willing to admit that women had a lot more to talk about than curtains and lipstick when they got together with their friends for brunch. Until the advent of the Internet put sex – virtual sex, at least – at everyone's fingertips. And until the advent of everything that informs the current zeitgeist, in which people talk about their sex lives, and the sex lives of others, with unprecedented openness, *ad nauseum*.

Now, I am going to be frank with you: although I try to maintain a veneer of unflappable tranquillity, I freely admit that talking about sex makes me feel a little bashful and red-faced too. But in the interest of serving you, dear reader, I'm going to grab the bull by the horns and help you to unpick some of these fascinating, sexy mysteries. While I can't promise that this chapter won't make you cringe once or twice, you do have my solemn vow that it will be less awkward than that time your mum or dad tried to explain it all to you.

But then, could anything not be?

The double standard: I'm a slut, you're a stud. Ick.

It was time for the Big Sex Talk. Alice was sixteen, going on seventeen. She knew that she was naïve, but quite in spite of that, she was spending rather a lot of afternoons pretending to do maths homework with her very first boyfriend in her very first boyfriend's bedroom.

And so it was, one bright spring afternoon, that Alice's well-meaning mother persuaded her beloved daughter to take a break from revising her maths, and took her out to tea. As her daughter chewed her way through a substantial slice of chocolate cake, Alice's mother tapped her fingers on the table, tense, before at last launching into a string of rather astonishing euphemisms.

'Sometimes,' Alice's mother said to her, forcing the words out with the determined articulation of a woman who had no desire to discuss sex but who would do it despite those major misgivings, because she had greater misgivings about becoming a grandmother in the very near future. 'Boys want . . . things.' She paused and sipped her tea. 'And . . .' she said, looking around the café furtively '. . . stuff.'

Most of us girls have been on the receiving end of a version of this monologue. If it wasn't our mother, it was an older sister, grandmother, aunt, teacher or (worst of all!) well-meaning male relative. In my case, it was my family doctor, who asked me at my school physical when I was fifteen if I was having sex, and then congratulated me with great enthusiasm on my valiant decision not to – not being aware that it was more of a default option than a decision in my case, due to my unsophisticated, nerdy adolescent lifestyle and strict, vigilant parents. While I am now perfectly delighted that I held off from having intimate relations with any suitors who were not yet old enough to drive, I am a little surprised that my doctor didn't also tell me that if I changed my decision (ha!) I shouldn't be afraid to ask her for contraception. This might have been a serious issue if I hadn't been such an unsophisticated and nerdy adolescent. But even in the relatively sophisticated climes of 1990s New York, it was still *de rigeur* to emphasise the value of preserving virginity to young women.

If you are male, in contrast, you are likely to have been on the receiving end of a conversation about the birds and the bees that was also awkward, but crucially different in content. It was probably not unlike the lecture that Jonathan received from his father:

> *Jonathan was thirteen. He was sitting in his bedroom, reading. Unannounced, his father entered the room, sat on the chair at the end of the bed, sighed heavily, said 'Um . . . just use a condom,' and walked out.*

What's the result of this? While few women actually go on to delay being deflowered until we get married, for many of us a slight feeling of unease lingers: when we have an unwise or disappointing sexual encounter (and who doesn't, once in a while?) the aftermath tends to include a feeling of guilt that I suspect is linked, in many cases, to a sense that we have compromised the virtue that adults told us to uphold when we were young, and that contemporary culture presses us to hold on to.

There have been many positive advances in terms of the degree to which female sexuality has been acknowledged and accepted by our culture. But a quick glance at the headlines at any newsagent in the UK will quickly confirm that we have failed to dispel the myth of the slut. This leads to all sorts of bizarre practices, such as women who repeatedly sleep with their ex-boyfriends because they want to have sex, but do not want to increase the number of partners they've had. Other women limit the range of their sexual activities to everything but intercourse in order to keep the number low: if a former president of the United States says it doesn't count as sexual relations, then surely it couldn't be. (Newsflash for those of you who, like me, came of age in the late 1990s: sociologists who study sexual behaviour disagree.)

In the course of my research for this chapter, I found one well-trafficked Internet forum where a group of newly-wed women were discussing how long they had waited until consummating their relationships with their now-husbands. Even though they had ended up getting married, almost all of the women who had slept with their partners within a few weeks of meeting them (which seemed to be pretty standard) punctuated their anecdotes by referring to themselves as 'sluts' or similar, as if they feared that the other women would judge them if they didn't acknowledge that having sex with their future husbands early into their relationships was evidence of low morals. This filled my heart with woe; even with the anonymity afforded by having the discussion online, these women still felt it important to refer to themselves as trollops, as if being a lady who enjoys sex with someone she loves is still a reason to be ashamed.

And herein, I believe, lies one of the major schisms between men's understanding of women, and vice-versa, when it comes to sexual encounters: on average, women tend to invest more emotionally in them, partly as a result of this kind of cultural conditioning, perhaps also partly as a result of the way that our genes are programmed to make us want to hang on to the men who father our children so that we don't perish in a cave (genes, of course, don't account for the role of condoms). But there are also times when, like men, women just want to have sex purely for pleasure.

But because this is still not considered to be completely socially acceptable, many women make a huge effort to trick themselves into feeling sad and filthy and used after having a sexual encounter with a man which was never going to be anything but casual. Many of us feel compelled afterwards to beat ourselves up about it if the man doesn't call, because that is what a nice girl should do – even though if he did call it would just lead to a brief, awkward, and wholly unsuitable relationship that might well involve actual emotional trauma. It's neither a good use of our time nor a way to develop a positive attitude towards our sexuality – which is, of course, crucially important to have when you do find yourself to be in a good relationship.

Sooner or later, love is gonna get you.

Jonathan: Alice, I know it is only our first date, but would you like to come home with me?

Alice: Absolutely not. On no account.

[Himglish translation: What kind of woman do you think I am? In fact I have intentionally not shaved my legs this evening in hopes of preventing myself from going to bed with you. I couldn't possibly sleep with you until we have gone out on eight dates. Because, you know, it said so in a magazine that I read once and I don't want you to think that I am a trollop. Even though, yes, I really do want to come home with you.]

Jonathan: Oh, thank goodness for that ... I mean, uh, yeah. Well, fine, whatever you want, I wouldn't want to pressure you.

[Femalese interpretation: Actually I think I quite like you, so I am pretty sure that I don't actually want you to have sex with me yet.]

Don't think for a minute that I don't realise that many men also struggle with their own set of gender-specific issues when it comes to sexual ethics – something which, I suspect, women are sometimes a bit hasty to overlook, which can lead to slightly comic (or tragic) consequences. My friend Will recently told me some advice he'd been given by a more promiscuous male friend when he complained that his love life hadn't been going quite as well as he might have hoped. 'He said that I should always try to sleep with a woman on the first date,' Will said. 'If I succeed, then I know that she's a slut and I shouldn't see her anymore, but I get to have sex. If I fail, then I know she's not a slut and I'll see her again. See? Either way I win!'

Will then furrowed his brow and looked sad, like he suspected that this was not really a very nice way of behaving at all.

You see, girls, it's also difficult for men, whose masculinity is often called into question – sometimes subtly, sometimes not – if they don't make attempts to initiate sex very early on. Because we assume that all men should be insatiable, that we should have to be gently removing their hands from our knees within the first half hour or so of a date, when they don't make at least a passing attempt to ravage us we tend to blame ourselves, assuming that they don't find us attractive or, if we have quite high self-esteem, that the man who doesn't want to sleep with us must certainly be homosexual. When you refuse to go home with this kind of man after a first date it is not a little bit amusing to see the relief wash over his face, if you can resist the temptation to call him on his disingenuousness.

My friend Paul is one of these. Whereas other men boast of their prowess at getting women into bed, Paul refers to his speciality as 'non-shagging'. By this he means the scenario that arises when he finds himself in a semi-intimate scenario with a woman who he knows expects him to make a move on her. Paul is a handsome, well-built rugby-playing man, but his exterior belies the fact that actually he doesn't care very much for casual sex. Indeed, he has become somewhat notorious for leaving a trail of frustrated and confused women in his wake, who blame themselves for their failure to end up in bed with him rather than it occurring to them that he might just be kind of restrained.

As a result of all of our attempts to conform, many of us end up going to rather stunning extremes in terms of the degree to which we engage in complicated, headwrecking pretences in the course of our courtships.

Jonathan: So, Alice, how many men have you slept with?
Alice: Hm. Let me see. One, two ... six ... seven ...
          does it count if it was really bad sex? Seven ...
          twelve, thirteen ... seventeen ... four. FOUR.
          And you?
Jonathan: What? Oh, me? I lost count. Obviously.

In 2007, some mathematicians in the US took a long, hard look at this phenomenon, and drew a rather surprising conclusion. (Yes, I know, mathematicians are not necessarily known for their outstanding sexual expertise, but don't underestimate them.) They demonstrated that when comparing the average number of sex partners heterosexual men reported having in a number of reliable British and American surveys, versus the average number of sex partners heterosexual women reported having in the same surveys, that it is logically impossible for men to have significantly more sex partners than women. In other words? Most of us are lying: men are beefing their numbers up and women are reducing theirs. (My number? Zero, obviously. My mother is reading this.)

But even though we all know that *we* are lying, we somehow think that it remains an important issue to discuss – especially those of us who are male. A quick poll of women I know confirmed the fact that men almost always ask us how many men we've slept with, for some reason. Apparently the most acceptable number is four: that's not so many that he will think that you are a lady of loose morals, but sufficient that he won't get all stressed that him sleeping with you means too much. Ridiculous. All of this is very tedious and, I think, is something that many of us would be wise to reconsider – if only in an effort for us to waste less of our time with unsuitable partners.

How soon is too soon?

The most popular and enduring arguments against women having sex early on in a relationship is that it is unlikely to lead to a lasting relationship: men, having satisfied their base carnal needs, will no longer value or respect the woman in question, and thus move on to the next one. Frankly, I don't think that these kind of assumptions are fair to anyone involved in a sexual encounter (or lack thereof). Most people would agree that we may know quite quickly after meeting someone whether or not we want to sleep with them: with men, my male friends assure me, the decision is usually made in a maximum of ten minutes; for women, it maybe takes a bit longer. Twelve minutes? As much as half an hour? Several weeks? I'm not sure. But in any case, it is important to keep things in perspective: if you have sex with a lot of people who you happen to feel like having sex with, the chances that you are going to marry one of them necessarily get smaller, not especially *because* you've had sex with them, but because the odds of finding that many people you are compatible with in the long- or medium-term are likely to be quite slim.

So I think we should relax, a little bit, when it comes to worrying about the determination of what is the right moment in a relationship to have sex for the first time. But I do think that it is interesting to consider how sex the first time you meet someone can create a particularly strange dynamic between the two of you, wherein you and your new gentleman friend may feel that you have a suddenly high level of carnal knowledge of each other that is not on a par with your emotional intimacy. I mean, if you sleep with someone with whom you would be hesitant to, say, discuss your political views or the fact that you like to eat hazelnut chocolate spread by digging it out of the jar with your hands and licking it off your fingers, for fear of alienating him, it is not surprising that regardless of your gender, bashfulness and awkwardness may ensue following early shared orgasms (or semblance thereof).

This is not an argument for not having sex, of course. I recommend having sex. I endorse it. It's healthy and fun! But it is, I suppose, an argument for considering the value of pausing before you jump into bed with someone new immediately, if you want to have the opportunity to develop your initial chemistry into a relationship that is actually good. Or else it is an argument for being really open and honest and up front about your most shameful secrets, no matter how disgusting they are.

> *'Hello,' said Alice to Jonathan as she sidled up next to him at a party. 'I often drool into my pillow, when I was sixteen I stole fifty pounds from my aunt to buy cider for all of my friends in the sixth form, and I really fancy David Cameron. You're terribly sexy.'*
>
> *'Lovely to meet you,' Jonathan replied. 'I pretend to be a non-smoker but actually just smoke other people's cigarettes a lot, I lie awake at night crying fat tears of heartbreak over my ex-girlfriend at least once a week, even though we split up over a year ago, and I cannot eat soup without slurping loudly. Shall we get our coats?'*

I shall leave it up to you to choose the most alluring option.

No, we're just friends who have sex. And kind of love each other.

As our willingness to commit to serious relationships has evolved in inverse proportion to our willingness to have casual sex, a new kind of relationship between men and women has emerged as one of the most common, and possibly most nefarious: the 'friendship with benefits' (FWB) or, for those of you who prefer to be coruscating and frank, the 'fuck buddy'. I don't think that this kind of relationship is nefarious because it is bad to have sex, but I do think that it doesn't have too much to recommend it because it is, in essence, an abnegation of responsibility by both the man and the woman, predicated on the assumption that as soon as something better crops up, either party can leave the arrangement without feeling any responsibility for hurting the other one's feelings. There are two key problems with this.

The first problem is that when someone better comes along, the beneficial friend must accept being relegated to non-sex buddy immediately. This is not so bad if you are having sex with someone you don't care about, but being a FWB implies that you do actually like your sex buddy (hence the word 'friend') – which means that you are likely to feel more than a little hurt when he or she gets into an actual relationship with someone else. We try to pretend that these little liaisons are just like any other kind of friendship that involves a shared interest, but sex isn't like Scrabble (thank goodness). If your special Scrabble friend finds a girlfriend, there's no reason why you can't carry on playing with his tiles. In contrast, continuing to have sex with your special sex friend is not OK, unless you really want to be someone's second-string sex partner. Is that what you really want? I thought not. You are much too cute and nice for that.

And second, I believe that because the FWB relationship has been so widely accepted as a reputable practice as opposed to a giant collective agreement to deceive ourselves, a lot of people, especially women, find themselves agreeing to get involved with a FWB because they are actually in love with the other (less enthusiastic) partner and reckon that a FWB relationship is better than no relationship at all. Of course, we do so gambling on the chance that the buddy will come around to the realisation that he loves us back. Guess what? He probably won't, because if he did, then he'd want to have a real relationship with you. And then when you finally confess your feelings, the parameters of your agreement with him will give him the moral grounds to accuse you of victimising him, or reneging on something that was perfectly clear between the two of you. It only ends in tears. If you are friends with someone and you like having sex with him, then you should probably just swallow your pride and your misgivings and have a full-blown affair. At least that way you'll be able to have genuine closure at the conclusion. Phoning up your friends to get them to commiserate with you when the person you have been casually, but consistently, shagging doesn't want to shag you anymore is difficult to do gracefully.

Scoring the goal: was it good for you, too?

Look back to ancient Greek and Roman civilisation, if you will, with their orgies and debauchery and relaxed attitudes towards homosexuality: though ancient, they had some views on the differences in sexuality between men and women which still serve as a rather piquant place for us to start our consideration of how the experience of having sex is different for men and women.

You see, according to those ancient Greek myth-makers, Tiresias was a blind prophet who (among many other adventures such as condemning Oedipus to fancy his mother) was metamorphosed into a woman for a while, in part to explore the mystifying question of whether men or women had more fun during sex, which was an issue that was being hotly debated between Zeus, the king of the gods, and Hera, his pleasantly cantankerous first wife, the goddess of women and marriage. After spending seven years living as a female, Tiresias returned to Mount Olympus to give his verdict: women, he declared, definitely have a better time. Zeus, having maintained that this was the case all along – 'You gain more than we from the pleasures of love,' he remarks in Ovid's *Metamorphoses* – was delighted to have proven his wife wrong and probably smirked in a godly way.

Pointless superstition, you scoff? Perhaps. But as any fifteen-year-old student of Classics knows, myths were coined not for entertainment, but because they had important social functions. They were invented to explain phenomena that couldn't be worked out in an era when scientists were still challenged to figure out tricky equations that would permit them to understand the relationships between the sides of a triangle, much less the relationships between men and women.

But here's the rub: it seems that maybe Tiresias, or Ovid or whichever orator invented him, might actually have been on to something. While it's always been quite clear what role the male orgasm plays in reproductive function, the utility of the female orgasm has been more difficult to pinpoint. Sure, the contractions can aid the travel of the sperm to the egg. Not to mention, of course, that women who aren't having orgasms may well be generally less interested in engaging in reproductive activity. But a woman can (alas) still get pregnant without climaxing, which means that some people – both men and women, mind you – go on regarding the female orgasm as somewhat optional.

But as it turns out, the gender difference in orgasms goes well beyond the facts of our respective equipment, to the neural level. In May 2008, a study published in *Scientific American* magazine indicated that brain scans taken while women were climaxing showed that 'at the moment of orgasm, women do not have any emotional feelings' – also described as 'widespread neural power failure'. Men's brains, on the other hand, were shown in the critical study to maintain far higher levels of neural activity when they came. If women's emotions aren't engaged when they climax, might one just argue that women are in it for sheer pleasure more than their male partners. On the other hand, couldn't it be that the male orgasm is designed in part to encourage a greater emotional connection between the man and the woman he is (if not using contraception) impregnating? That's better for the species, no doubt. And thus, while other studies seem to have demonstrated that sex may have greater emotional resonance for women because we are biologically programmed to hope that it leads to children and commitment, it also is apparent that to a certain extent when it comes to orgasms, the sheer pleasure that a woman experiences may subsume that of her male partner . . .

. . . If a woman has an orgasm, that is. The myth that the female orgasm is a myth has, happily for all of us, been unequivocally filed away in the archive of Archaic Sexist Things. But less happily, a surprising and sad number of women still find that coming doesn't, well, come easily to them. According to the BBC (and who doesn't look to the BBC for one's sexual healing, in addition to incisive coverage of sport and news) 12 per cent of women never climax, ever (!) and moreover 75 per cent simply do not climax from having intercourse, contrary to popular misconception that a failure to do so indicates that a woman or her lover (or both of them) are inadequate.

I will now tell you a true, embarrassing story about myself. It is one that I am reluctant, but willing, to share because I care so much about you all. I did not have an orgasm, ever, until I located my clitoris, and I located it just as I somewhat nerdishly figure out most things: I looked it up in a book.

The book, in this case, was *Gray's Anatomy*, and I highly recommend that if you have any confusion about the way you or the woman in your life is wired – and you might, considering that as recently as 2008 scientists in Italy were cheerfully announcing that after years of research they had actually discovered the female G-spot (and of all the people in the world who one might have thought had sex sussed prior to that, wouldn't you have thought it was Italians?) do go to your local library and have a quick look. You may just find it is elucidating: knowledge is power, people. And OK, maybe you will also find it a little embarrassing, if you've been getting it a little bit wrong for some time, but no one can fault you for making an effort to improve your technique, whether you are yourself in possession of a clitoris or dating someone who is.

And furthermore, my dears? If after all of this research and inspection of diagrams and pleasant practice, it is still impossible for you to communicate with your partner about your sex life, then maybe you need a new partner – not just because he can't communicate about sex, or because he is hopelessly prudish, but because the odds are that you are going to be inclined to get your wires intractably crossed outside the bedroom as well.

Faking it.

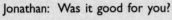

Jonathan: Was it good for you?
[Femalese intepretation: I'm not very aware of the experience you're having here, but please confirm my sexual prowess.]
Alice: Wait, was it supposed to be? Oh. Ohhhhhh! Yes, in that case, of course, sure, yes. You're the best I've ever had, or, you know, whatever.
[Himglish translation: Um, maybe you should do some more, ah, research.]

Now, of course, no discussion of the female orgasm is complete without a discussion of the issue of the fake one. Remember how I noted earlier women's general tendency to feign things a lot more than men, because we are so conditioned to avoid hurting the feelings of others at all costs? Well, naturally, this also applies – perhaps especially applies – to bedroom activities. I did a quick survey of some recent examinations of this phenomenon in the scientific press, and although the research methods vary significantly, the aggregate conclusion appears to be that as many as 70 per cent of women admit faking orgasms with their present partner. And this doesn't, of course, take into account their past partners. And it also doesn't take account of the fact that the women were probably not interviewed under ideal circumstances for being frank about their sex lives – which would be while slightly intoxicated and surrounded by their close female friends. So I am going to go out on a limb and say that, well, few women have not faked an orgasm at one time or another.

Not always being able to come is not something to be ashamed of: the fact is that there are always going to

be times when even the most dedicated and loving minis-
trations of our most simpatico gentleman friends just don't
quite do the trick. Ideally, in an established relationship, it
is not so much of a problem: you should be able to gently
explain to your long-term other half that it's just not
working, that you love him anyway, and would he maybe
like to have a cup of tea instead, without making him feel
devastated and awkward. Fine. But it can often be quite
difficult to reach that level of comfort and trust with
someone. So it is the stages before we reach that level
when we find ourselves driven to fake it.

But whether you are male or female, of all of the
contents of your bag of sexual tricks, the faked orgasm is
kind of an unfortunate one. It is almost always employed
only in states of panic. Despite its apparent handiness it
is, in the long run, a serious strategic mistake. It is not
unlike going around to someone's house for dinner and
being served something awful. Out of a fear of hurting
feelings, most of us respond to this kind of scenario by
lavishing the chef with the kind of false praise that can
only guarantee that we will be on the receiving end of
many future unpalatable servings of the same dish: 'I made
your favourite!'

While this kind of dishonesty is utterly well meaning,
it isn't particularly good for either the host or the guest:
it will only get harder over your repeated culinary suffer-
ings to express to the chef that he is failing to serve up
what you really need. And this will only make him reflect
on all of the other times you've gone into paroxysms of
false excitement over his technique. He will feel squirmy
and mortified and is unlikely to invite you round for dinner
ever again, even though the courses that came before dessert
may have been consistently terrific.

So, girls, if someone you're having sex with is repeatedly

trying but failing to make you come, you really must swallow your fear of hurting his feelings and tell him, even demonstrate, if you hope to carry on seeing him.

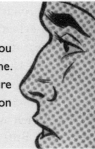

Jonathan: Was it good for you?

Alice: It was nice. But, actually, it would be great if you did something a little bit different next time. Have you ever read *Gray's Anatomy*? Just by pure coincidence, I happen to have a copy here on my nightstand.

You should explain it in your very best Himglish, so that he understands: fight your desire to use euphemisms that don't actually clarify the problem (or the fact that there is a problem). Most men want to be genuinely bringing women pleasure as opposed to merely having them make fake noises of the sort that they believe is appropriate to the situation, and thus they should be open to a little bit of discussion – a man who isn't should, perhaps, stick to onanism. And girls, even if you don't think that the two of you have any future together, consider letting him know that it's going a bit wrong as a humanitarian gesture: if you're not going to see him again, then it hardly matters if he is a little bit miffed, and at least then his future lovers will not also have to suffer through that weird, awkward thing he keeps doing to your earlobes.

The Internet is for porn.

Less than a decade ago, when I turned eighteen, I went home on a break from college to visit my parents and some of my friends from school. Ian and I went to the local video shop to rent one of those new technological innovations, a DVD. 'Jean,' he said, solemnly, 'now that we are both eighteen, I have to show you something.' He led me through a small door labelled 'Adults Only'. I had noticed it before, but I had always assumed that it would lead to a small pornographic closet, so my mouth fell open in amazement and horror (I was a well-brought-up child) when I saw that the square footage devoted to pornographic videos was actually greater than that of the rest of the video store.

I was astounded. But I probably shouldn't have been: I am part of a generation that has had easier access to pornography than any before ours, thanks to the advent of the Internet around the time that we hit puberty. In 2008, an informal survey on the website Jezebel led a multitude of women to report their shock at brand-new partners asking them to submit to a manoeuvre commonly found in porn. While it's something that some people, according to preference, might consider to be reasonable behaviour for consenting adults, many of the women found it to be a horrifying suggestion in the early stages of a sexual relationship. Or, indeed, in any stage of a sexual relationship – as my friend Julia remarked upon hearing this graphic little survey, her face twisted into an expression of abject horror: 'Not the first time, not the hundredth time!'

Of course we all know that men have been enjoying porn since it occurred to some seminal cave artist that it would be quite funny to etch a phallus on the wall; it's widely accepted that they are more easily aroused by sexual imagery (or other visual stimulants) than women, who are less image-oriented and find aural stimulation more sexually piquant.

The statistics on how many men actually consume pornography and with what frequency remain highly contentious and variable, particularly depending on whether the survey is being conducted by their mums or by the lads they play football with. But it seems that when it comes to using pornography, men do so at rates that are three or four times higher than women, depending on the country in which the statistics were taken. Basically, it is safe to assume that with a few exceptions, most men are consumers of pornography at one point or another in their lives, and they consume it quite a lot, whether they are actively standing on their tip toes to buy the most special-interest top-shelf magazines or they are being somewhat more passive in their consumption, flicking through an issue of *Playboy* supplied by their barber (my male friends in university found one such provider of haircuts early on in our first year and were henceforth far more well-groomed than most students rightfully should be).

But contentious statistics aside, thanks to the Internet, the fact of the matter is that pornography has affected our sex lives in recent years more than it has ever before. It's not too complicated: online accessibility has meant that in the last ten to fifteen years, boys who once would have needed to rely on plundering some ancient collection of magazines belonging to an elder male relative have had an infinite selection of graphic images at their disposal as soon as they could figure out how to do a web search for 'Hot Babez' or similar. Now, subscriptions to *Playboy* are down – the company reported losses of a million and a half pounds in the first quarter of 2008 – but traffic on sexually explicit sites remains buoyant. Indeed Internet pornography, at the time I am writing this book, remains the most profitable product on the World Wide Web. Hm.

It's a difficult thing to measure through anything but anecdotal evidence, but it does seem quite likely that our expectations of the mechanics, the aesthetics and the dynamics of sex are increasingly affected by the vision of the people who write and direct and produce pornography rather than our own experiences. That's not just the case with men, either: women are also looking at porn, although not with quite so much enthusiasm as their male counter-parts – albeit, perhaps, with greater frequency since it started being stocked on every high street in Ann Summers. Pornography has been increasingly accepted as something that long-standing couples will employ as part of their normal, healthy sex lives – although one wonders if it is quite right to do that when it is likely at the cost of the normal, healthy sex lives of the performers (which is a debate, perhaps, for another book). But the market is increasingly expanding to include directors who profess to create pornography that is designed to appeal specifically to women, who feel less shy about admitting that they are not averse to being turned on by sexually explicit images, but who fail to appreciate the awful misogyny that is so often a strong motif in mainstream pornography.

In any case, because of this tremendous profusion of porn, the tropes and motifs and trends of the genre (I think it is quite charitable of me to describe it as such) are leaking over into mainstream media and entertainment. Fashions for women being completely bare down below (necessitating having all of their pubic hair ripped out with hot wax), setting up stripper poles in their front rooms and snogging other women in crowded bars because they know it excites male onlookers (and not because they particularly fancy the other women) were all common motifs in pornography before they became quite dull, middle-of-the-road activities.

Now, whatever your views on the usage of pornography, whether you think it is awesome or foul or somewhere very grey in between, it is clear that its penetration into culture changes our expectations of sexuality and can be a source of major stress when it transpires that we are rarely able to achieve the sexual 'norms' that pornography sets. Sex is enough of a challenge for women (and, admittedly, men) to engage in without us feeling that we have to live up to these sometimes twisted (and twisty, in a yoga kind of way) expectations. I think it is time for us to put our collective foot down: we can't ban anyone from consuming pornography or media inspired by pornography entirely, if only because it's difficult for anyone to avoid it completely without cutting yourself off entirely from the mainstream. But we shouldn't fear being condemned as prudes or sluts if we make it a point that we will be active and equal partners in bedroom activities, and that sometimes that means that the act that he has been fantasising about ever since he saw it on the pay-per-view channel in a hotel will remain a fantasy as far as we're concerned.

Taking the surgical route to good sex?

Here's what I know about surgery: I had an appendectomy at the age of fourteen and it was an excruciatingly painful experience, both in terms of the actual pain – if you can avoid ever having a scalpel slice through your stomach muscles, then please do – and in terms of the sheer indignity. Multiple shots of morphine and pills the size of horse tranquillisers sort of helped with the physical pain, but only the passing of the years has alleviated the mortifying aspects of the rest of the experience, from having to pee into a measuring cup to wearing really ugly, sweaty surgical stockings, to being made to limp around the ward by a cheery nurse who seemed to believe the embarrassment of being seen in a flapping hospital gown was no reason for me to refuse to join her on jolly walks to help me regain use of my bedridden, atrophying limbs.

I offer you this little digression not to garner your sympathy for my long-ago suffering, but rather to under-line my concern that hundreds – nay, thousands – of women are voluntarily putting themselves through similarly unpleasant surgical experiences. And not because they have nearly explosive appendices or other medical problems, but because they are unsatisfied with the appearances of their breasts or genitals, so convinced they have been by the strange discourses that tell women that our bodies must conform to the impossible, airbrushed objects presented to us by the media.

I'm not a particularly weepy lady in general, but the thought of women being so concerned about the appear-ances of their vaginas that they get bits of them trimmed off in an effort to make them more attractive makes me want to cry. While there are certainly uncommon instances in which this procedure – labioplasty – may be required to maintain a woman's sexual health, the frequency with which surgeons are performing them on women who have no problem other than anxiety about the appearance of their vaginas is rapidly increasing. In fact, it is the fastest-growing cosmetic procedure in the UK: the National Health Service reported that twice as many of the procedures were performed in 2007 than in 2006, and that doesn't account for those which are done privately – at costs of several thousand pounds that, if you believe British tabloid papers, a fair number of women are cheerfully borrowing from credit cards and mortgage brokers in order to finance. This continues to be promulgated despite warnings from respected gynaecologists who have indicated that insuffi-cient research has been carried out to confirm whether the procedure is safe or in any way useful in terms of its effect on female sexual function.

So why then, when this all sounds rather dubious, are women putting themselves through this? It's somewhat ineffable, but it seems not unlikely that as the ever-expanding availability of sexually explicit material in the media (and particularly in pornography, as I mentioned before) may have altered sexual practices, so it has altered – or perhaps skewed – impressions of what body parts should look like.

But do you want to know the most ironic thing about all of this flesh-trimming that's going on? Men, besides those who are plastic surgeons and who are actively trying to get you to pay them loads of money to perform surgery on you, just do not remotely care what your labia look like. And I'm not just saying this to make us all feel better: while we know that men are more inclined to become aroused due to visual stimulation than women, and although they may be known for being detail-oriented in other areas of life, they're actually not when it comes to sex. Dozens of surveys have found that men are completely indifferent to the issue, perhaps not least because by the time they have the opportunity to have intimate knowledge of a vagina, they are quite distracted from aesthetic considerations by more pressing issues. For heaven's sakes, ladies, if you are really insecure, just ask.

Alice: Jonathan, what are your thoughts on my vagina?
Jonathan: Excuse me?
Alice: I mean, do you think it looks all right?
Jonathan: This is the most bizarre conversation we have ever had. Can we just have sex now, please?

By the time you get the words out, you will realise just how ridiculous it is: the vast majority of men will respond by looking at you in confusion, and then saying that they think that you are perfectly wonderful just as you are. And you know what? They will not be lying!

But, of course, don't think that we girls are all alone in our collective neurosis about the appearance of our genitals. I get at least six advertisements about penis extension and enlargement on a daily basis, and I don't even have one, so I imagine it is even worse for people who are actually in possession of the things. Men – or boys, no doubt, in changing rooms at school – invented genitalia comparison. But while women may jocularly discuss the question of whether size matters, most experts agree that few relationships have ever been terminated solely because a man's penis was under- (or over-) sized. When we really like – or, indeed, love – someone we are, as a human race, surprisingly good at making accommodations to have sex with them even if they are not straight off some kind of assembly line. But despite this we are more inclined to assume that if someone doesn't want to sleep with us it reflects badly on us, instead of on them for having bad taste in the opposite sex.

Let's be frank, kids. Vaginas? Not always nice to look at. Penises? Most often a clear victory of function over form. But does it matter? No. Psychologists who specialise in sexual dysfunctions rarely deal with people who are suffering from relationship problems because of the size or the shape of their naughty bits. Despite our suspicions that when beautiful people do it, it is glamorous and different, we all know deep down that sex is quite often a bit bizarre and bodies are funny and weird and we are all quite uniquely assembled. And yet the majority of us, despite our deviations from the supermodel norm, still manage despite our myriad minor deformities to have sex. And sometimes it's rather great; sometimes it's rather regrettable, but the greatness or degree to which it should be regretted is not determined by the trimness of your labia or the length of a man's shaft.

My advice to you? If anyone ever suggests that they would enjoy having sex with you more if your sex organs were a little prettier, and if you would be so kind as to endure a traumatising surgical procedure in order to make yourself a tiny bit more attractive and thus somehow more worth their company, I highly recommend that you should never have sex with them again.

Fuck 'em. Except, don't.

In summary . . .

Himglish: Sex is complicated. Don't feel ashamed if you don't want to have it once in a while, and don't be surprised if it's not good if you're not interested in communicating with your partners.

Femalese: Sex is even more complicated for us than it is for men, but it's complicated for them too. Consider what feels right for you, and pursue that – irregardless of whether your behaviour conforms to particular ideas or expectations that are laid out for you by the culture you live in, your social group, or something that you (or someone you are sleeping with) saw on television. And unless you have a serious medical problem, you do not need surgery on any part of your body to help you have a better sex life. OK? OK.

4

Commitment: I Will Love You For Ever. I Guess

As far as the twenty-first-century romantic meeting of happenstance goes, it couldn't have been any more text-book. I got in touch with Roderick for professional reasons via a mutual friend, and we started emailing back and forth. The emails became increasingly banterful and, I daresay, a bit flirtatious; he finally remarked that he simply couldn't go on with our correspondence without meeting face to face. He suggested that we get together for a drink. Having taken the necessary measures of carefully examining Roderick's photographs on Facebook to figure out if I might possibly fancy him, and consulting with the friend who introduced us in the first place ('He's smart, and tall, and also rich,' she said, with just a small hint of glee), I agreed to meet him for a cocktail, a week hence. It was an ambigu-date, to be sure – had sparks not flown when we met, then there was still space for us to write it off as another boring professional networking session. But considering that there wasn't actually any professional reason for us to meet, since the project was complete and there wasn't any prospect of future collaboration, I was quite sure that Roderick's intentions were more date than ambigu.

Anyway, in the interim: at a party that weekend, I met a nice woman who, as we chatted away, happened to mention that she knew Roderick. Coincidence! I said to the nice woman. I had met him because he was giving me a hand on a project I was working on, I explained. And in what context did she know Roderick? The nice woman looked aside, sipped her drink, blushed in a pretty fashion.

'Well,' she said. 'Roderick and I . . . we're dating, actually.' The nice woman giggled, in the manner beloved of schoolgirls. 'It's only been a couple of weeks, but he's really romancing me.'

'Me too!' I wanted to say. But I didn't, because my strong desire to be courteous has an irritating way of overriding my almost-as-strong desire to live in a Woody Allen film.

It will not surprise you, dear readers, as it didn't surprise me, that I never heard from Roderick again, for I suspect that he might have worked out that his jig was up. It was slightly disappointing, really, as going through with our meeting would have been interesting, and fantastic for research purposes. Sigh. But I never waste an opportunity, my dears: this incident makes for a good jumping-off point for thinking about the nature of commitment, or, rather, how men and women may have differing views on commitment.

In this particular case, I think that if I had told the nice woman at the party that I was scheduled to go out for a drink with the man who was romancing her, she might well have felt hurt and betrayed, and maybe even felt that he was cheating on her. But Roderick might well have been under the impression that really romancing someone for only a couple of weeks placed him under no imperative not to meet other women for ambiguous drinks.

And furthermore, of course, the contemporary parameters of male–female interactions would have given him a stronger leg to stand on than hers, in many respects.

The fact that it is perfectly OK for a man and a woman to meet in a hotel bar in the evening to drink cocktails and discuss their jobs without any scandalous implications would have provided him with a fine alibi if his self-appointed girlfriend had found out and been unhappy. On the other hand, most women believe, painful as it is, that they should resist the urge to bring up the issue of exclusivity for as long as possible for fear of terrifying men and causing them to seek shelter from their terror in the arms of other women.

But would either Roderick or the nice woman who he was really romancing have been incorrect about the state of their relationship, or lack thereof? Of course not! As is so often the case with matters of the heart, the apportioning of blame is impossible when it comes to two people grappling over the issue of a definition of commitment that makes sense for both of them. Regardless of what we think we learned about true love from reading fairy tales when we were little girls, or even from listening to what the vicar instructs us when we recited our wedding vows, each relationship is like a snowflake. A lopsided snowflake, that is: individual, delicate, and – compared to any kind of model snowflake that you might fashion out of tissue paper to hang off your Christmas tree – jagged and weird. But just because it is jagged and weird doesn't rule out the possibility that it can be a remarkable and beautiful thing.

It's one thing to negotiate the inherent challenges of finding someone you like, as we've already examined earlier in this book, but it's quite another to take that person you like and get him or her to stick by you indefinitely – or, for that matter, make yourself stick by him or her. But it's mostly him, of course. Or is it? According to some of our most beloved stereotypes of the rules of romance, the process of achieving commitment in a romantic relationship is an intense battle of wills between the desperate-to-be-locked-into-eternal-devotion woman and the reluctant-to-cease-sowing-his-wild-oats man. Indeed, the chances are quite strong that the very shelf you plucked this book from in the 'Relationships' section of the bookshop was otherwise heaving with several quite humourless manuals offering instructions on how to best secure (and keep) a husband.

Thank goodness you opted to read this instead. I'm not interested in following the trend of trying to develop some kind of complicated, ostensibly infallible algorithm [frilly apron + submissive 1950s attitude − sex = Husband (Diamond ring)] that will ensure that you will be able to dupe or coerce someone into a committed relationship with you.

Nope! Instead, in this chapter, we're going to discuss if, and how, and why, men and women view commitment differently. And then we will consider how these differences might best be reconciled, without requiring anyone to be manipulative or over-compromised or withhold sex in the interest of compelling their other half into signing on to a shared mortgage or agreeing on a wedding date. And I daresay, before this chapter draws to a close, we might just take a moment to celebrate the fact that modern girls can afford to be a wee bit more independently-minded, a bit more true to themselves as individuals, than all of those stacks of pink-spined paperbacks seem to think we should be. Does that all sound quite good? Yes, I think so, too.

It's not you, it's his Y-chromosome. Or is it?

Why is it that we assume that men are anti-commitment? To a large extent, of course, this assumption is based on their role in the reproductive process. Yes, in theory chaps can love you and leave you and feel assured that their genes will be propagated without them giving much thought to the small human that results from the loving and leaving, while they move on to seek the next fecund lady for further propagation. While, fortunately, that is not what most men seek to achieve in this day and age, yes, it is possible.

But I don't think that regarding this as a default stance for most men is very fair, or wise. It stems, of course, from an assumption that we make decisions based on our unmitigated primordial urges, as if we are dwelling in some kind of unsocialised vacuum or Hobbesian state of nature. We're just not. In fact, as we learned in the last chapter, heterosexual men, on average, don't actually have vastly more sexual partners than women – it is just not possible. Furthermore, few people would deny that men who are interested in engaging in their children's upbringing are now not particularly exceptional, even though research shows that they have yet to shoulder an equal burden to women when it comes to child-rearing. And, of course, children don't even remotely come into the equation in a lot of relationships that last for a very long time. So basically? We can't blame men for being reluctant to commit on that basis.

Another common argument holds that the incentive for men to settle down is now low because it generally requires them to make economic compromises – since statistics show they will make more money than their female partners. Perhaps. But as I will point out in the chapter on domestic bliss, it has been demonstrated that men who are cohabiting or married live longer and are physically and mentally healthier than their single comrades. In the long run, I'd argue, this means that the additional costs of a wife or girlfriend – bouquets of flowers, your dignity when she makes you go to the shop to buy her some tampons – are quite a small price to pay.

And yet the stereotypes endure, and the men don't commit. Why? To a certain extent, I think it is because they buy into this old-fashioned binary too, that commitment is some kind of strange battle in which they are supposed to resist and women are supposed to beat down their resistance. And they buy into this just as some of them (though they might be loath to admit it, bless their little hearts) also accept, to some extent, the legend that real men maintain their real-ness through going through women like they go through fast cars, that they will somehow be sacrificing some kind of alpha maleness if they concede that they could actually love a lady, that sometimes it would be quite nice to go through life with a partner they could count on. *Ils sont un peu pathetiques.*

'I wasn't asking for anything,' a friend of mine said recently, in a state of rather extreme distress over her rejection by a soulless cad. 'I wasn't being clingy or demanding at all!'

Therein lies a serious problem faced by the modern woman: many of us have become so thoroughly convinced that nothing is more off-putting to a man than a sense that he is being encouraged to commit, that we have driven ourselves into a corner where we allow them to control the pace of relationships without our input, for fear that any expression of preference on our part will drive them away. This is, of course, pure, unadulterated bullshit.

Let's face facts, girls: a man who really likes you will be genuinely interested in what you want – for example, he'll respect the fact that you might like to have the opportunity to see him sometime when you are both not hammered beyond belief. If he responds to this kind of suggestion with horror or discomfort – well, darling, I'm sorry to say that he is just not the one. But isn't it a good thing that you took the initiative and worked that out for yourself, rather than continuing to try to endure his indifferent and disdainful treatment of you? A useful rule of thumb: would you allow a female friend to treat you this way? Would, for example, you accept her assertion that she can only see you after midnight because things might otherwise be too serious? No, you wouldn't. You would say that she is crazy and you would probably stop being friends with her. Just because you are having sex with someone (or want to have sex with someone) doesn't mean that you shouldn't expect to be treated with the same degree of human kindness that you expect from your friends.

Above all, I have come to believe, in this especially self-obsessed era in which we are dwelling, that the male fear of commitment is most strongly linked to a fear of the death of identity: of becoming 'Alice's boyfriend' instead of Jonathan; of becoming part of a unit; of a loss of agency or free will. Though this has always been something of a consideration for men entering into a committed relationship, in a culture in which self-improvement and individual achievements are so highly valued, it's not surprising that men who have reached the kind of age when people might expect to settle down sometimes panic at the prospect. As far as they can see, rather than being elevated into a sort of alpha state of leadership of their families as traditional marriage once promised them, commitment just means that they'll have to compromise even more than previous generations of men had to.

It can sometimes make for a somewhat dire game to play for those girls who find that without wanting to go into 1950s housewife mode, they wouldn't mind a bit of stability in their lives, perhaps even some kids. Thanks to all of the ambiguity that swirls around the status of our relationships, being aware that it is now considered to be more socially awkward to say, 'I'd really like to get married' than to say, 'I'd really like to have a threesome with the postman and my yoga teacher', many of us have been reduced to grasping at pathetic straws that might be construed as indicators of commitment. Saying, 'will you be my girlfriend?' can be awkward and scary for the average speaker of Himglish, so they tend to avoid saying it all; bereft of any other way of gleaning the information, distracted by the rush of affection, of the stage that her relationship is at, the lady who is fluent in Femalese is inclined to start looking elsewhere for validation.

I'm as guilty as the rest of you. One time, for example, I got quite excited when a man I'd been dating for five or six weeks and rather adored invested in hypoallergenic pillows so that I didn't have a violent asthma attack every time I spent the night in contact with his bedding, which was generously stuffed with the feathery remains of what seemed like a thousand battery chickens. Touched beyond belief by his pillow-purchasing efforts, I did the obvious womanly thing: I told my friends. He bought me pillows! I told them. Hypoallergenic pillows! The girls and I all agreed it was terribly adoring and a definite sign that he was definitely my boyfriend. Celebration all around. (I think some of them may have started shopping for hats to wear to my wedding.) Oh, romantic!

Except that, of course, maybe he just bought the pillows not just because he wanted to show me how much he cared but also because he was displeased at being kept up at night by my laboured breathing, and found it inconvenient to stay at my flat. I had to consider that this was possibly the actual reason for his trip to IKEA, when he ended our nascent relationship ten days later, leaving me heartbroken and wondering whether I should refer to him in future as 'ex-boyfriend', 'guy I dated for a while' or simply 'wheeze-inducing'.

There is something awfully unromantic, and a little bit too pragmatic – not to mention a little bit teenage – about having what is popularly known in New York as the define the relationship (DTR) chat:

Alice: Jonathan, we need to talk.

Jonathan: (Bristling in anticipation of some kind of admonishment) Didn't we just talk yesterday?

Alice: Yes. We need to define the relationship. What am I to you?

Jonathan: (Tapping her on the nose with a forefinger): Adorable!

Alice: That's not the point.

Jonathan: (Confused) Isn't it?

Alice: We're been dating exclusively for three weeks now. You even let me touch your crème brûlée torch. So am I your girlfriend?

Jonathan: Hm. Well. I mean, yeah, OK. I guess. Does this mean you'll go on the pill and we can stop using condoms when we have sex?

Alice: (Taking what she can get) You're wonderful, Jonathan!

(They embrace passionately.)

There's no need to have conversations that sound like a badly scripted soap opera if you can help it. But for the woman who is lying awake at night wondering whether the man in her life will commit to her, there is definitely something to be said for checking in, every now and then, to confirm that you and the object of your affection are on the same page about what the parameters of that affection are. Indeed, it can be helpful to do this whether you're a guy who is resistant to settling down, a girl who's already set a date for her wedding and needs only to secure the groom, a man who's dying to find someone to take his last name or a woman who is committed to independent living and having a string of lovers. Because few things are worse – not just passion-killing, but just plain dispiriting and maybe even devastating – than making the discovery that you and your partner are in two totally different relationships, albeit with each other.

She's the one, but does she want to be the one?

For women, desiring a lifelong committed relationship was long a matter of economics as much as it was about biology or emotions or a genetic predisposition for wanting to (figuratively) grasp a man by his nether regions and never let him go. Unmarried women were far less well-off than their married peers (and still are in many societies), both in terms of finances and social advantage. We may now take our relative freedom for granted, but until quite recently there wasn't much space reserved in Western society for women without permanent male partners, and the space that was there was popularly known as 'on the shelf' or, worse yet, we were referred to as 'spinsters', which wouldn't be a nice word even if someone figured out a way to make it mean 'adorable puppy' instead of 'undesirable woman incapable of catching a man'.

As a result, women started envisioning their weddings at the age of eight and panicking at the age of eighteen (or fourteen, in certain US states) if it became apparent that they'd not yet secured a likely candidate to march down the aisle with them, father their children, support their lifestyle and generally give them a reason to live. Of course, there were always many women who actually weren't terribly keen on this kind of arrangement, but who ended up committing themselves, and their husbands, to unhappy marriages because they really had no other option. The social rules were simply so rigid that it took a great deal of mettle and determination to stray outside their parameters. 'Twas better, quite often, to be locked in a loveless marriage that at least offered a modicum of financial stability and social status, than to be a single woman.

Alice and Jonathan's best friends, Maisie and Toby, were getting married. Alice was serving as the maid of honour, and to that end, had accompanied Maisie to the bridal salon to assist her while she tried on dresses. Sporting ten kilos and ten thousand pounds worth of lacy fluff and a frilly curtain tied to her head, Maisie gazed, teary-eyed, at her reflection in the mirror.

'Oh, Maisie,' Alice couldn't help but giggle a little at the sight of her friend in the hideous, eighties-esque cupcake costume, the kind of garment that she would shudder to even be seen wearing when she was dead. 'I just could never imagine myself wearing that.'

'Don't worry,' said Maisie sweetly. 'I am sure that Jonathan will propose eventually.'

Things have changed, haven't they? Although women are still, on average, making substantially smaller amounts of money than our male counterparts (something I shall discuss later on in the chapter on office life, among other things), we not only have more opportunity than ever before to pursue careers regardless of our marital status; we're expected to, even if everyone thinks that we are on the brink of being married to the heir to the British throne.

And like our male counterparts, we don't want to give

up our sense of identity either: we don't want to compromise on our careers, we don't want to take a supporting role in someone else's life if they're not willing to reciprocate, we don't want to change our surnames (unless we're old-fashioned or the one that we inherited from our dad is a bit crap). Girls of my generation are frankly very lucky, I think, that the scales have tipped just enough – just – that it is often accepted that it is not necessary for a woman to have a male partner in that man-as-commodity or man-as-accessory kind of way, as much as it is nice for her to have a male partner if she finds someone with whom she is quite compatible. We don't even have to be monogamous if we don't want to: sure, it is something that many people continue to strive for, but we are increasingly accepting of the fact that a single monogamous relationship is not necessarily satisfying for everyone.

And yet, although we're putting it off until a later age than ever before – the average British woman is twenty-eight when she gets married, and that's younger than the average continental European woman – we are still entering into wedlock. The important thing to keep in mind, however, is why we are entering into it – because we want to, because our partners want to, and not because all of our friends are doing it and we feel inadequate that we haven't managed to do it yet, or that we've reached an age where there aren't really any milestones left, and it must be fun to have a wedding, so hey, current boyfriend, you'll do. That can be harder than it sounds – much as I don't particularly care to look like a cupcake, even an independently-minded lady like me knows first-hand the little sense of wobbliness and insecurity that sometimes penetrates a woman's tough-cookie exterior when she finds herself sitting in a pew for the nuptials of yet another one of her contemporaries. 'A woman needs a man like a fish needs a bicycle,' wrote Irina Dunn quite famously, but even she ended up married.

The fact is that even though it is getting easier, it is still harder to be an unmarried woman of a certain age than to be an unmarried man. The former are perceived to be sad cases who can't have sex because they don't have a special man in their lives; the latter are seen as paragons of fun, because unlike other men who have been entrapped into unnatural monogamy, the single man can continue to indulge his desire for infinite choice as long as he cares to (longer, these days, thanks to Viagra).

I don't usually advocate looking to Hollywood for useful illustrative examples, but in this case I think collective attitudes towards our perceptions of men and women, and the role that committed relationships play in our lives, is quite interestingly summed up by the experiences of George Clooney and Jennifer Aniston. Clooney has had a string of long-term girlfriends over the years since he first became a bona fide sex symbol in the early nineties, with his starring role on *ER*. He's frequently professed that he's not ever going to get married again and that his heart will always belong to his now tragically-deceased pet pig. Aniston became famous for her role in *Friends* around the same time that Clooney rose to fame. She is ten years younger than Clooney and has also been married and divorced once, and she has for years been photographed out and about on her own looking perfectly cheerful, with accompanying captions to the photos explaining how her life is one of empty solitude due to the fact that in public, at least, it is apparent that she has been unable to sustain another long-term relationship since her divorce (a divorce which the press seems firmly convinced was due in part to her refusal to have children with her ex-husband Brad Pitt, despite rather more compelling evidence that it was because he had an affair with his current partner, Angelina Jolie). Sure, Aniston has had a successful career and is, like Clooney, extremely rich, and though she has never expressed public passion for a pig, it appears that she does have a very nice dog. But despite having roughly the same trappings of what makes for a good life for Clooney, Aniston just can't be left to enjoy her good fortune in peace, because too many people accept that it would simply not be possible for a woman to be beautiful, rich, healthy, forty and happily not married.

And thus, we girls start believing that too, instead of believing our own instincts. What does this lead to? Well, low self-esteem, for one thing; marrying quite the wrong person, for another. In many cases, we even end up making stupid pacts with our male friends when we are twenty-five and lonely and have had too much to drink, agreeing that if we are both forty and unwed, we will get married simply for the sake of not dying alone. It's a righteous shame and I applaud women – and men – who stand proud and single and lead rich, happy lives without capitulating to the norm which dictates that happiness requires that you be constantly accompanied by a member of the oppo-site sex. Sure, it can be very nice to be accompanied by a member of the opposite sex through life, but the bottom line is that we should feel comfortable being happy as indi-viduals – which, incidentally, is a state of mind you probably should be in before you try to make a long-term relation-ship work, even if it's with your back-up husband.

It's complicated. I mean, really complicated.

Just as it has profoundly changed other aspects of our personal lives, our newish friend the Internet has brought a whole new facet to the nature of commitment, with our almost frantic use of the web to inform the wide world of the details of our personal lives through a variety of different mediums, but particularly via social networking sites such as Facebook. When you sign up to join one of these sites, you're asked by default to share your relationship status. For some of us, it's a no-brainer; for others, especially those in ambiguous relationships, it can kick off an existential crisis.

from: *Alice Femalese*

to: *Jonathan Himglish*

subject: *status*

Jonathan, I've noticed your FB profile relationship status is set to 'It's Complicated.' WTF?

xxx

from: *Jonathan Himglish*

to: *Alice Femalese*

subject: *Re: status*

Ha ha. I thought that was quite funny, sweetpea. I mean, weren't we just discussing the other night how all relationships are complicated?

xxxxxxxxxx

from: *Alice Femalese*

to: *Jonathan Himglish*

subject: *Re: Re: status*

God, Jonathan, this is serious. Do you really want people you went to school with when you were twelve and haven't spoken to since to think your relationship is complicated? Change it! (I am signing off without kisses because I'm pissed off and want to electronically imply that I no longer love you after this brief exchange. That's not complicated.)

from: Jonathan Himglish

to: Alice Femalese

subject: *Re: Re: Re: status*

FFS!!!!!!!

:-(

In the spirit of primary social research, I altered my Facebook status so that it sent round an announcement to my several hundred Facebook friends (a group that includes some of my actual friends and quite a few people I once knew in high school) that I was 'no longer in a relationship', despite the fact that I hadn't been in a relationship in the first place. I shortly received several curious, sympathetic messages. The first one arrived minutes later from my neighbour Harry, who lives a floor down in my block of flats and whom I see several times a week. Harry was well aware, in light of the numerous times I had sat on his couch with a cup of tea in hand and analysed my most recent romantic disappointments with him, that I didn't have a boyfriend to break up with. But nonetheless, like so many of us, Harry's brain has been wired to respond in a Pavlovian fashion to the sight of that little red broken heart. If Facebook says it is so, it's the truth. Apparently, Harry reckoned, I must have been concealing a secret liaison that had crumbled . . . one that I apparently felt compelled to announce on the Internet but not in a personal conversation. Hm. That sounds totally crazy when I write it down, doesn't it? But in light of the fact that more than eleven million – *eleven million* – people in the UK have Facebook profiles at the time of writing this book and the fact that Facebook is the second most popular website in this country after Google, it is apparent that rather a lot of us have accepted this kind of craziness into our lives.

In Facebook, as in life, it appears that women are more eager to publicly declare their romantic affiliations than men – we tend to be the one that takes the initiative to click on the fateful box and hope that our beloved will follow suit. Being in a relationship gives women status: the Facebook relationship is kind of a twenty-first-century version of a promise ring or a fraternity pin, except that it is much, much less expensive.

And also, unlike these tokens of commitment, which involve the man passing off one of his belongings to the woman he loves (this permitted him to not actually have any symbol to indicate that he wasn't free to love whomever he chose, thus enforcing his macho-ness), the Facebook relationship is more even-handed, in a way. It requires that the man has to own up to being enamoured as well. And most significantly of all, the Facebook relationship is a token of commitment that is imparted with meaning because of the sheer publicness of it – more so, for example, than that other important token of contemporary togetherness that is the clear STD screening. In a sense, I suppose, it shows yet another way in which modernity has not stopped us from expressing our primordial instincts: marking our territory is important to us. And perhaps in the current era of partner-swapping, of chopping and changing, of an apparent dearth of long-term commitment, these kinds of public tokens of togetherness mean more to us now that neither men nor women can necessarily count on the kinds of special gendered tricks – a fat wallet, an intact hymen – that used to make us desirable.

My first instinct is to say, 'Whatever, Facebook!' It's difficult to predict, of course, whether we'll all be rampantly Facebooking in ten years, or if we will have moved on to another form of communication, but it does seem quite clear that there is a trend of putting an increasing amount of what was long considered to be one's private informa-tion out in the world for public consumption is here to stay. Like getting toothpaste back in the tube, it appears to be very difficult to revert.

Because of the sheer penetration of social networking into, well, our society, I don't think it is possible to completely dismiss it. What it is possible to do, however, is to take it with a grain of salt. It's so easy to get caught up in the idea that there is some kind of universal stan-dardised measure of commitment that, as I pointed out before, this overlooks the reality that every committed rela-tionship is a special snowflake. Maybe your boyfriend is happy to tell the world via Facebook that he is your boyfriend but won't introduce you to his mother; perhaps your boyfriend maintains that he won't commit to being labelled as permanently yours online but is perfectly happy to hang out with all of your friends. Which scenario is better? No one can say. And that's fine.

Together 4-eva.

There's no denying that I am strongly influenced by the example set by my parents when it comes to my personal views about commitment and, in particular, the possi-bility to succeed at it in the long term. Over three decades of a marriage that has sometimes fallen short of perfect bliss (the last time I went on holiday with my parents, aged twenty-four, I had to have a little shout at them from my seat in the back of the car when I couldn't stand hearing them bicker over directions any longer), my mum and dad have nonetheless handily supplied me with one example of how to establish a long-term commitment in which both parties are pretty happy. And being in such close proximity of this model has certainly given me a confidence in the sustainability of a really long relationship that I am well aware not all of my peers actually share – or, indeed, would have any grounds to share. There are more children of divorce in my generation than of any preceding it, and in keeping with the example set by our split-up parents, many of us take the concept of 'till death do us part' with quite a large pinch of salt, even if we still think getting married is a good idea.

And it is not just relationships that we no longer have the same imperative to commit to. In the chapter on dating, I touched on the issue of how the explosion of choice in every aspect of our lives affects our relationships in the earliest stages; it may even have a greater impact on us when we're assessing the possibility of a romantic long game. Going out with someone for a few weeks is one thing; agreeing to an arrangement that is indefinite or even ostensibly meant to be lifelong quite another thing – a tremendously daunting thing.

What else in life do we commit to for that length of time? Not our careers: where it would once be perfectly normal for someone to sign on to a corporation when they were twenty-two and bid farewell over forty years later, these days it's rare for anyone to last much more than a decade before they get itchy feet. Not our homes – British eighteen- to thirty-five-year-olds are projected to move home an average of ten times in their lives (by the age of twenty-four, I was already up to eight). Though love is obviously a different matter entirely, it maybe is not entirely surprising that our collective tendency to chop and change other things in our lives leaks over into our love lives, too. We're so used to getting what we want that we're loath to settle for anything that falls short of ideal.

But is this realistic? I am inclined not to think so. I'm not simply extrapolating from the giant divorce rate;

I'm reckoning, instead, that it is simply quite unlikely that many of us will have the good fortune to find that elusive member of the opposite sex who doesn't make us roll our eyes once in a while; indeed, someone who from time to time we don't find rather loathsome (hopefully not for very long periods of time).

But there is a surprising person who sums this situation up even better than I. I am almost ashamed to tell you who it is, so ardently uninterested am I in anything that involves hobbits or rings or wizards, but anyway: J.R.R. Tolkien. Yes, the author of *The Lord of the Rings*. Yes, that one. Wrote Mr Tolkien, in 1941, in a rather prescient fashion that makes me almost think that I should consider giving Bilbo Baggins a second chance (only almost, though):

> Nearly all marriages, even happy ones, are mistakes: in the sense that almost certainly (in a more perfect world, or even with a little more care in this very imperfect one) both partners might be found more suitable mates. But the real soulmate is the one you are actually married to.

In other words? Your partner is probably not a perfect person. (Unlike you, especially after you finish this book.) But it's the person you've picked, and if you have reasonably good taste, he probably has a lot going for him. In Yiddish there is a nice, romantic word, *bashert*, which refers to the concept of predestined romance. I'm not so sure about that. Rather, I think you can find your *bashert*, not necessarily because you cross the street in front of them at exactly the right cosmic moment, but because you, as two people with free will, mutually decide to be each other's *bashert* – it's an ongoing, dynamic project, rather than a state of being that is hewn in some kind of metaphysical cement.

Though we may be more inclined to harbour romantic dreams of Mr Right when we are young, I think that women are much quicker on average to accept the reality of the non-perfect partner, perhaps because of this enduring belief that we should have to settle down one day. In contrast, some men seem to continue to regard anyone but the perfect Miss Right as a potential limpet who will deprive him of his sense of self. This latter attitude is one that more and more women seem to be adopting as we become more confident in our capacity for blazing our own trails through life without depending on male assistance or support.

Now, here's the thing: if you are concerned about losing your sense of self because you are in a committed relationship, then by all means don't get involved in one – I mean, really, *don't*, as it is so very unfair and not a little bit cruel to the other person who is involved. Don't even pretend to get involved in a committed relationship (we shall discuss this in more detail forthwith). But if it happens repeatedly, then I think that whether you are male or female, you would be wise to take a moment, or maybe a lot of moments, to ponder the question of whether the committed relationship is really the problem, or your lack of confidence in your own self-determination could actually be an issue.

And sometimes, finding or defining ourselves can be a rather ineffable – and ultimately, extremely tedious – goal. It is something that men often feel they have longer to do, because the counting-down of their reproductive clocks is not nearly as rapid. And thus we women find ourselves feeling all racked with jealously sometimes at the spectre of our male contemporaries failing to feel an imperative to settle down before they are forty and instead enjoying the trapping of a hugely extended adolescence well into their thirties.

Will they be sorry when they are middle-aged and all alone? Those of us who have dated twenty- and thirty-something men who seem to think citing their extreme youth is a viable reason to avoid committing to more than an occasional shag with their girlfriends probably like to think so. There is simply not a magic time, anymore, when we know that we are unequivocally adults, but maybe both men and women would be happier if we were to acknowledge that staying young at heart and committing to share that young heart with someone special are not completely incompatible activities.

Boys and girls, I certainly don't advocate surrendering yourselves to relationships that are totally horrendous, but relationships that are occasionally mediocre? There's really very little else in life from which either men or women feel justified in demanding perfection. When your job is less enthralling than it was initially for a few months, you usually don't march out and find a different job, especially if you still have some confidence that sticking with it will pay off in the long term; if you have a fight with your mother and sulk and don't speak to her for a couple of weeks you usually don't start looking for a new mother. So should we not be a bit more at ease with the fact that there are times when our relationships will be rubbish and we will have to work quite hard to make them less unpleasant? Yes, we should. Because that is commitment.

In summary . . .

Himglish: The woman in your life may well think that you are more committed to her than you actually are. Be prepared. And, um, maybe don't be afraid to grow up?

Femalese: Do you want a boyfriend? That's fine, but there's no need to be hasty about it unless he is the right one. You are absolutely brilliant on your own, and you mustn't, under any circumstances, forget that. Sometimes things that you believe to be signs of commitment actually aren't, in man-world. But while placing the blame on men for not wanting to commit may sometimes be accurate, it's not productive and may result in you spending far too much time at home, clad in pyjamas and owning cats. Instead, you must assert yourself and figure out how to get what you want without fear of overstepping boundaries.

5

Domestic Bliss: Hey Honey! I'm Home (Break Out the Crème Brûlée Torch)

Now: show me a person who doesn't quite like a good wedding, and I will show you a person who is not very much fun. Though there can be quite a fine line between a wedding and a Las Vegas extravaganza, it's hard not to love an event which centres around avuncular dancing, massive quantities of chicken, and a woman wearing a giant white dress that weighs more than she does, and which requires her to employ the voluntary servitude of a small team of pastel-clad ladies in order for her to be able to disrobe enough so that she can pee.

If you are a hopeless romantic, the typical twenty-first-century wedding is a beautiful opportunity for two people who love each other to pledge their undying commitment to that love in front of an audience of people who love them, too. Or, if you like your romance a bit less hopeless and a bit more practical, the typical twenty-first-century wedding is a beautiful opportunity for two people who love each other and have already pledged their undying commitment by becoming co-signatories on a rental agreement or a mortgage, to assemble the people who love them in the interest of hosting a grand soirée, and the acquisition of a great deal of very high-quality kitchen equipment.

We have strayed very far from the days – not so very long ago, of course – in which the typical modern wedding was the beginning of something completely unfamiliar to the people standing before the altar. How fondly I recall one time when I was in college, aged nineteen or twenty, discussing my dream wedding, as young women are apt to do (at the time I longed for a bridal dress that strongly resembled a Baked Alaska, a dream that you will be pleased to know that I have since abandoned) with my friend Thea. Thea was a worldly girl. While I pondered what kind of flowers my bouquet should be composed of when I at last convinced my then-boyfriend that in fact he could learn to love me more than he loved hot salt beef sandwiches, (he dumped me not long afterwards but still, as far as I know, loves those sandwiches) Thea was more interested in the carnal implications of getting hitched.

'Imagine,' she said, her eyes sparkling with ribald amusement, 'what it must have been like when people were actually virgins before they got married! There must have been all kinds of tension in the church, with everyone watching them and thinking, "They're about to have their first bonk!"' I laughed the knowing, cosmopolitan laugh of a woman who had had sex at least six and a half times. What a preposterous prospect!

But, of course, there's a lot more to marriage than sex. Not only have most modern brides and grooms got their first bonk out of the way long before they do that special rhythmic marching down the aisle that the solemnity of matrimony compels a lot of people to do, most of them have also had first-hand experience of the myriad adventures that abound from the experience of living with a member of the opposite sex. While those born in the first few decades of the twentieth century still shuddered at the prospect of inter-gender dwelling when fingers were sans rings, some of their children took bold strides to explore pre-marital cohabiting thanks to the license for, ah, licentiousness provided by the 1960s. And now, the current generation of young adults – and, indeed, many slightly older adults who are on their second round in the commitment game – have embraced it wholeheartedly.

While some may bemoan this trend as evidence of deep rents in our social fabric, I think that it is probably pretty smart: the prospect of making a lifelong commitment to someone we've never cohabited with now seems incalculably foolish. Indeed, foolish even if it does mean that the fabled excitement of being carried (or carrying someone) across the threshold of one's post-nuptial home can all too easily become de-glossed when the first thing you clap your misty newly-wed eyes on is a pile of dirty clothes that your beloved fully intended to sink into the laundry basket before leaving for the wedding, but instead left strewn across the bathroom floor. But is this kind of forced intimacy with your partner's gym socks before you have pledged yourself to him for life not but a small price to pay for the confidence that you are actually compatible when it comes to this cohabiting lark?

In Britain, particularly rampant enthusiasm for the pre-marital shack-up amounts to about a quarter of men and a quarter of women under sixty living with partners to whom they're not married, which is twice the rate it was in the mid-nineties. And rates of pre-marital cohabiting are even higher in free-loving continental Europe. And why not? Living expenses are prohibitively high when it comes to maintaining individual households, and social barriers to living with one's partner (e.g. neighbours peering through their net curtains to see whether you are wearing a wedding ring) are low – quite often, as a result of this, couples find themselves living together without quite having made a conscious decision to do so.

Alice had been dwelling in Jonathan's flat for three weeks before he noticed that she was actually living there. It started, as these things do, with an innocent toothbrush.

'Here you go,' he said, the second time she stayed over, in an attempt to be chivlarous. 'This green toothbrush can be yours.' Alice beamed, for, as women do, she knew full well that to be given her own toothbrush was the first step on the road to matrimony.

Next was a drawer, after they'd been together for a month or so.

'It's dreadfully inconvenient having to carry this large bag containing a change of clothes and my hair straighteners out to dinner every time I meet you after work,' Alice remarked. 'Sigh.'

'Would you like a drawer?' Jonathan said, magnanimous and drunk on love and a nice Shiraz. 'Have a drawer.'

Three months later, the drawer was overflowing a little bit.

'Do you live here?' said Jonathan one morning, thinking he was being facetious, as Alice went through his laundry to find some clean underwear.

'Yes,' said Alice.

Jonathan looked back at her, with a raised eyebrow.

'Didn't I tell you?' Alice smiled sweetly. 'My lease ran out three weeks ago. Do you want me to look for a new place?' She blinked at him: big, limpid, innocent blinks.

'Er,' said Jonathan. 'Er, of course not, this is fine for now . . . until you find a place.'

'Until I find a place,' said Alice. 'Yes. Of course.'

It is not at all uncommon. You think you're going to have a big heart-to-heart chat about the stage your relationship is at and whether you want to take it to the next level of commitment, but heart-to-heart chats are actually quite awkward. Then someone's lease runs out or plumbing goes haywire, you're sleeping together every night anyway, and before you can say 'Shall we ring the estate agent, darling?' you find that you have been ensconced in unexpected domestic bliss for months. Oops.

There's a lot to like about living with your loved one: sex on tap, no more arguments about whose flat you'll return to after an evening out, someone to keep you from leaving the house in the morning looking like you've been dragged through a hedge backwards. But perhaps we should be putting a teensy bit more thought into a scenario that can also have a significant downside. A variety of studies have found that cohabiting couples are far more likely to split up than married couples – up to twice as likely, in some cases – which in many cases results in all the fun of going through a divorce and subsequent emotional trauma/resentment/fear of commitment, without any of the fun of acquiring the expensive kitchen equipment to fight tooth and nail over in the split.

And just because we're more anxious than ever to shack up with members of the opposite sex, it doesn't necessarily mean that the nuts and bolts of cohabiting have become any easier. Anyone who has done it knows that the establishment of a happy mixed-sex household is by no means merely a matter of working out who should take responsibility for doing the washing up and taking out the rubbish: the achievement of domestic bliss (or the distinct lack thereof) can be a profoundly different experience depending on your sex. Not to mention how much sex you're having with the person you're cohabiting with, since our newly relaxed society means that so many of us are happily opting to live with members of the opposite sex upon whom we have no romantic designs. Or, you know, romantic designs that we're willing to admit.

Cohabiting: is it good for you?

Our grandparents, and our parents, likely felt pressured to settle down and get married in order to conform to social expectations for normal adult behaviour. But we are increasingly – and I daresay somewhat blissfully – able to reject such social norms and form lasting relationships for more selfish reasons. This is not to overlook the fact that many young (and not-so-young) people still must deal with weighty expectations of people other than themselves when it comes to selecting a mate, but with more people in many Western countries living independently than ever before, our collective imperviousness to the old-fashioned reasons to couple up has clearly increased. Of course that doesn't mean that we're not still often inclined to settle down. But in light of the unprecedented agency we have to make independent decisions about who we love, how we want to establish our lifestyle with them, and whether we care about making our relationships legal, it is clear the potential drawbacks of cohabiting have to be outweighed by the benefits. You will not be surprised to learn that figuring out what those costs and benefits potentially are can certainly be strongly influenced by our gender. Men and women both benefit from living with each other, but in many respects they benefit in different – and not always entirely complementary – ways.

It's not very fresh news that marriage has been proven to have many health benefits – we've known for quite some time that people in marriages are statistically likely to live longer, have better physical and mental health, enjoy greater financial stability than their unmarried peers and – perhaps the most remarkable benefit of all – don't have to suffer the stress of trying to impress their friends with lurid tales of their impressive sex lives because no one expects them to be having sex at all anymore. But what about the sinful shacker-uppers?

Well, not surprisingly, the kind of experience that you have in this scenario does depend a lot on your gender. For women, this means that if you are wondering why the hell your live-in boyfriend of twelve years has yet to produce an engagement ring, you may want to consider that it's not because he is a cheapskate or harbouring some kind of outlandish phobia of committing to you. In fact, a number of studies conducted over the course of the last few years have demonstrated quite unequivocally that simple, sinful, pre-marital cohabitation works out well for men. It seems that living with a woman significantly improves their mental health – they have lower rates of anxiety and depression than single men, but also than men who are married, which apparently indicates that not only do blokes do best with cohabiting, but that in relative terms, they don't do nearly as well with more permanent commitments.

You ring-witholding men, however, might be wise to consider that if you are feeling that your live-in girlfriend is exerting undue pressure upon you to make your relationship legal, she is simply attempting to pursue the option that will be best for *her* well-being. The same study that identified that cohabiting men are in many ways better off than their single or married peers, also demonstrated that women are mentally healthier in marriage – perhaps, the researchers postulated, in part because without the financial incentives that marriage provides women, they suffer from increased stress and instability. Furthermore, women's stronger nurturing instincts (thanks, primordial sex traits) have long been thought to fuel a greater desire for the establishment of the unparalleled security that a wedding licence offers.

And perhaps because of these factors, women just do not do as well as men when it comes to recovering from shattered relationships. Men are just much more resilient when it comes to recovering from break-ups with women and getting involved in new relationships. Could this be because ultimately commitment means less to them? Perhaps. In contrast, researchers have found, it is not necessarily better for a woman to have loved and lost than to have never loved at all, but rather healthier for her not to have had a relationship in the first place if it was doomed to end in floods of tears. In fact, particularly in cases where women have experienced a series of broken serious partnerships, they are probably better off just skipping the love and, you know, being busy and interesting and taking evening classes. Of course, it also doesn't help that, post-split, women are far more likely to end up financially worse-off than their former partners, particularly if there are children involved.

Now, hang on a second – are you thinking what I'm thinking? Of course you are: this appears to be a properly sticky wicket. But does it mean that we all must accept that men and women can't really ever live together and be happy? You will have noticed by now that I don't really ever think that the easiest or most mediocre option is worth settling for – and, hey, men and women have lived together (albeit often tempestuously) for a rather long time. So: tell your partner what you want, even if that is to live in a cupboard on your own; find out what he (or she) wants, and figure out a way to find a happy medium, rather than an unhappy one. If you want to get married but he still wants to live in the cupboard? Fine. What's important is that you find a way to strike a balance that works for you and your partner and makes both the male and female halves of the couple feel not just happy but mentally healthy, even if everyone who knows you thinks that you are a bit weird.

Damn it, sweetie, roll over!

Now, after reading the above I imagine that any of my female readers who are living in sin, or who have at least been pondering it, might be feeling slightly discouraged. But although cohabiting may improve their overall health, there is one major way in which living with women is frequently quite undermining to men. There's no shame in admitting it, girls, even though it makes us sound a bit soft: a lot of us like to have a bit of a cuddle after sex. One study conducted by a sexual lubricant company found that 80 per cent of women actually prefer cuddling to sex altogether, although I would wonder if that data was slightly skewed by the survey respondents' feelings about the prospect of employing that particular lubricant. In any case, most women agree that snuggling makes us feel warm and secure and lovely with the right man, especially since it causes our brains to produce lots of nice oxytocin.

But our male partners are not always so keen on the chaste-but-loving snuggle, thanks in part to the neutralisation of the oxytocin in their brains by the coital gush of testosterone. It makes them less inclined to want to continue to be in contact with their lovers, in addition to the burst of serotonin that they get after sex which makes them fall asleep. But though we may bemoan this behaviour as evidence of men's intrinsic callousness, it turns out that it is not fair to blame cuddle-aversion (entirely, at least) on the assumption that men are less in touch with their emotions than women and can easily detach associations between love and sex. In fact, a 2008 study found that when they sleep in a shared bed, men significantly lose out on sleep as a result of being disturbed by the presence of their partners.

While in interviews the male subjects of the study claimed that they hadn't been disturbed, tests of their cognitive function revealed that their brain power was notably impaired after co-sleeping as opposed to sleeping alone, and that stress hormones were elevated. So perhaps we should have a bit more sympathy in the morning after our boyfriends burn the toast and forget how we take our coffee: slumbering next to us, it seems, makes them a little bit stupid. Morning-after Scrabble, honey? Shall we place a small wager on it?

But as you lie awake at night, chaps, staring enviously at your girlfriend as she snoozes away, don't be too angry: you must also consider another 2008 study which determined that, due to the vacillations in their body temperature which are linked to the menstrual cycle, women have more nightmares than men – nightmares which may not actually cause them to wake up, but which do render sleep less restorative. So she may be getting more sleep than you, boys, but that sleep might well be a decidedly stressful experience.

Do you want to see my crème brûlée torch?

Jonathan and Alice invited their friends, Maisie and Toby, around to their flat for dinner.

'Dinner was delicious!' Maisie said to Alice, helping herself to another spoonful of organic mashed potatoes and celeriac seasoned with hand-churned butter and some very ancient and distinguished Parmesan cheese.

'Don't thank me,' Alice said, with a tight smile. 'Jonathan did all the cooking. He cooks, and I do the washing-up afterwards.'

'Cooking is my passion,' Jonathan beamed with pride.

> He winked at Alice. 'I'm really quite domestic, you
> know.'
>   'Apparently,' said Alice, with a distinct lack of a pride-
> filled beam, 'doing the washing-up is my passion.'

Our expectations of how the home is run have changed significantly in the last few years, haven't they? A 2008 American survey found that women are taking charge of more household decisions than ever before, in contrast to previous studies in which men were shown to be the key decision-makers: in some cases, women were even getting the opportunity to share the television remote control equitably with their husbands. Emasculating! But in an interesting twist, just as women are getting to break out of the kitchen, men are claiming it for themselves. We're in the throes of a new era of male domesticity – or, as I like to call it, *domistericity*. No longer must women feel like they are being harsh or unfeminine to expect that the men in their lives (and in their homes) need to participate in the running of their households. And as a result, even the most strapping heterosexual chaps are taking on household duties, applying their task-oriented brains to the challenges presented by the typically female realms of cooking and household hygiene.

There has been a remarkable change even over the course of my lifetime: when I was in primary school, 'homemaker' was the option that most of us wrote with respect to our mothers on the questionnaires that asked us about our parents' occupations, because it was somehow supposed to be more dignified to call them that than 'housewife'. I had every reason to expect that when I grew up, I would also be in charge of the housekeeping and the 2.4 children and the dog. But now that I actually am grown up, the prospect that any man I should ever have kids with would expect that of me is perfectly appalling – and judging from my established lack of passion for making my bed and pairing my socks, that's an awfully good thing. But what's quite interesting about this, I do believe, is that men who have chosen to embrace domistericity don't hesitate to apply to some of these dull aspects of housekeeping that particular brand of masculine enthusiasm – the male competitive streak – that we are familiar with from a number of different realms, from the football field to the animal kingdom.

It's even spread to the older generation, where domestic dynamics have shifted significantly. My own father, born during the Second World War with nary an expectation that he should ever have to learn to wield a dustpan and brush, has taken this project on with the same characteristic aplomb that he applies to more masculine undertakings like mowing the lawn and watching sport on television. After more than thirty years of happy marriage to my mother, Dadelstein has developed the kind of enthusiasm for baking bread and hoovering the carpets that might well qualify him to be a top-flight scullery maid, should he decide, post-retirement, that he wishes to take a new career path. And Dadelstein is certainly not alone: clubbing beasts is no longer an option for men who wish to prove their manly worth, and in many cases, although they continue to outstrip women on the earnings league table significantly, even a large paycheque may not quite suffice to confirm their status.

Could it be that a flair for the domisteric is the new key to being an alpha male? Many chaps seem to think so. Indeed, even the world's most powerful man seems aware that it is important that he should demonstrate that he is just as at home in the kitchen as he is in the crisis room. In an interview with the American news programme *60 Minutes*, broadcast just ten days after his election,

Barack Obama sat next to his wife Michelle and beamed as he told the journalist how much he likes to help out in the kitchen.

'Sometimes it's soothing to wash the dishes,' he said.

'You?' responded the anointed First Lady, in weary, sceptical Femalese tones that will be familiar to any man who has ever embellished the truth in an attempt to impress someone in the presence of his wife. 'Since when was it ever soothing for you to wash the dishes?'

'You know,' Obama replied, exuding, as always, unparalleled charisma, 'when I had to do it, I'd make it into a soothing thing.'

Though I acknowledge that the sample I am referring to might be drawn from a slightly specialist pool (bookish, inclined to sport tweed trousers and ironic plastic-rimmed spectacles and ride about on vintage bicycles) I've been surprised of late by just how many men I encounter who, no doubt having absorbed some important life lessons from the likes of Gordon and Jamie and Nigel, boldly attempt to impress me through boasting of their culinary skills on the first or second date.

'I call it "fuck fish",' bragged one friend of mine of his speciality dish. 'It looks impressive, and it's light, so then the women I cook it for don't feel too full and still want to sleep with me afterwards.' (Um, no thanks, honey, all of a sudden I'm not hungry.) Women used to know that the way to a man's heart was through his stomach; now men have taken on board the rule that a display of even quite rudimentary culinary skill is the way to a woman's knickers.

In contrast, as much as we may muddle romance up in other ways, if there's one thing that all girls know for certain in terms of the rules of dating, it is that unless we are going on a date in the 1950s, we should not discuss our domestic fantasies in the initial throes of a romantic liaison.

Equal to the lack of hesitation that the average modern woman will display if she feels like jumping into bed with a new love interest is the lack of enthusiasm that she will display for jumping into the kitchen in the early stages of romance, for fear of appearing retro and desperate and attempting to trap someone into a lifetime of miserable commitment. One might as well present the man in question with a shepherd's pie with 'Please love me and be the father of my children' written in elegant ketchup script across the mashed potato topping.

For those of us girls who do enjoy cooking as much as the next guy, it doesn't seem completely fair that we've lost our former dominance in the kitchen, but if the trade-off is the right to aspire to a greater freedom from domestic drudgery in the long-term, I suppose that we can't complain too much. While previous generations may have depended on their ability to snag husbands simply through demonstrations of their ability to look after their homes (and by proxy, their husbands) we no longer have that luxury. Instead we rely on other facets of our personalities: our sparkling intellect, our sense of humour, our good grooming, our ability to drink pints. Is that such a bad thing? I'd rather spend a couple of hours chatting about politics or books or creepy Channel 4 documentaries than sweating over a hot stove in an attempt to impress someone.

But, then again, it doesn't seem quite fair that men can get so much romantic capital from something that women have been in charge of for so long, simply because the sight of a wooden-spoon-wielding be-aproned gent is somehow still considered to be unusual, and a sign of particular sophistication. For as much as modern men and women are supposed to be dividing domestic responsibilities into neat and equitable halves, certain expectations have died hard: we're not impressed when women admit to domestic prowess, because deep down we have not been able to collectively reject the premise that it should come naturally to them. And the converse – we are convinced that men who are just as adept (or probably more so) in the kitchen as they are in the garage are doing something that is exciting and quirky and a little bit subversive in a sexy way.

Thus they extol the virtues of Nigel Slater and decry Jamie Oliver; they lure innocent women into their beds by cooking them fragrant cassoulets and push aside the contents of the stereotypical bachelor refrigerator (tall cans of domestic lager, two kinds of ketchup, something that may once have been delicious but is now rendered unidentifiable by mould) in order to fill it with impressive stocks of organic Jerusalem artichokes, locally grown turnips, and illegal unpasteurised cheese (I once shared a house with a man who was so partial to the latter that the stench kept me awake at night and I had to make him put it out in the garden).

In my twenty-sixth year of life, I came across three men – *three* – who had in their personal possession crème brûlée torches and Le Creuset cookware for which they provided the kind of loving care – polishing, buffing, affectionate stroking – that previous generations of boys devoted to their jalopies. And not only were they not ashamed to admit it, all informed me solemnly that they had these particular pieces of equipment in their kitchen arsenals within hours of us making our initial acquaintance – it was all, 'Would you like a drink? Let me tell you about my cast-iron, porcelain-lined saucepan.' One of my suitors even actually emailed me a photograph of his thick-walled casserole dish.

In fact, a display of cooking skill is now so valuable to the single man that some are willing to outsource the task if they aren't capable of it themselves: my friend Ben, a righteous cook, actually found himself pressed into service by his boss like some kind of culinary Cyrano de Bergerac after the boss had promised to present the woman he had recently started dating with a lovely home-cooked meal – despite the fact that he was himself a devotee of things that were frozen or came from kebab shops. But there was a caveat, Ben explained: 'He asked me to leave something that he could chop in front of her to make it more convincing.'

Truly amazing. But before you get hot under your collars, gents, (which you have starched and ironed all by yourselves, of course) because I have poked fun at your culinary prowess please realise that I think it is great that men can cook. It's perfectly heartwarming to see that you, too, are choosing to live against the suffocating dictates of outmoded gender stereotypes.

Alice: Jonathan, there is something wrong with the bathroom.

[Himglish translation: You left the toilet seat up again.]

Jonathan: Really?

[Femalese interpretation: I am lazy and unobservant!]

Alice: How many times must we go over this? No one can enjoy the aesthetic value of the fluffy toilet seat cover if you do not neatly replace the lid.

[Himglish translation: Seriously, I love you but you are actually a moron.]

Jonathan: Oh. Well, it is difficult to keep in mind when I am so often distracted at home by your inability to park the car without leaving two of the wheels on the kerb.

[Femalese intepretation: Now I will counter your criticism with a legitimate one of my own! See, I'm not a total dimwit.]

But it is important to note that men's newfound enthusiasm for being dominant in the kitchen does not mean that they are totally off the hook: we simply cannot overlook the fact that the women in their lives are still doing the lion's share of the housework. The statistics are elucidating to the point of being a little shouty: amongst married couples where both halves work full-time, the most recent studies have shown that women who share their households with male partners still do an average of about 70 per cent of the domestic duties after a long day's graft in the office. Unmarried cohabiting men are a bit more helpful, which seems to indicate that couples tend to shift into more traditional roles after they've actually tied the knot.

That isn't very much fun for us girls at all – not even a diamond the size of the Ritz can outweigh the appeal of having someone to actually split these onerous tasks with fairly. And when I say onerous tasks, I'm not referring to interesting DIY adventures, although I am sure that I am not alone in appreciating the surprising enthusiasm boyfriends of mine have shown for doing things like reattaching loose doorknobs and bleeding radiators, which they somehow seem to regard as a suitably masculine challenge. DIY is a lot more satisfying than dusting, my male friends, but dusting still has to be done, and it has to be done more often, and if you do it we will actually be much more inclined to let you maintain your obsessive and mildly disturbing relationship with the remote control.

So while women who have no interest in reheating soup may well be benefiting a great deal from the domisteric enthusiasm for demonstrations of culinary aplomb of their male partners, we are, in general, also still shouldering most of the burden when it comes to the myriad forms of housework that do not lend themselves quite so well to creativity and self-expression. But we go on doing it because somehow, for all of the excellent work of the feminist movement, we can't quite shake off the expectation that women assume responsibility for household maintenance as a default and men only do it if they are particularly, extraordinarily evolved (or metrosexual, if you prefer that term).

Having a boyfriend present us with a nice fresh bowl of *vichysoisse* is all very well, but for a man to show a willingness to make the bed, to sweep and mop, to keep the bedroom in the kind of order that he applies to the organisation of his preferred electronic gadgets? That, dear chaps, is what really makes us go weak at the knees. And furthermore, convenience be damned: if you live in a household that is entirely comprised of men, you must leave the toilet lid down anyway: for reasons of aesthetics, for reasons of hygiene – do you have any idea what kind of germs get sprayed around when a toilet is flushed while open? You don't want to know. And you might as well also put it down in the hopes that one day a nice girl might actually come round to your house to visit.

Now, of course I am generalising – before my male readers (I know you are out there) start writing me angry letters, I certainly acknowledge that there are quite a few very special men who are outstandingly tidy and who can wield a mop like the average mum wouldn't believe possible. And often women can be equally bad about defaulting to stereotypes when it comes to the performance of certain household tasks. I once shared a flat with several people including one super-neat man called Jake, and I never realised how brilliantly super-clean he was and how rottenly spoiled I had become until I moved into a new, all-female flatshare. After a few weeks, I noticed that the carpets weren't cleaning themselves and that if I tied up the rubbish in the bag and left it by the front door, it didn't grow legs and walk out of the flat (although it

certainly grew other things). Oh. Jake, I suddenly understood, probably found my reluctance to take the trash out
mildly irritating. And though we remain friends to this day,
I imagine he will always think of me as the girl who was
incapable of picking up a bag of rubbish. We probably should
have talked about it. But we didn't, sadly. As with all of
these gender-y misunderstandings, the only way to strike a
balance at the end of the day is a rousing discussion.

My love don't cost a thing.

Jonathan: The electric bill is here, and it is really expen-
sive this month.
*[Femalese interpretation: You use your hair straighteners too
much.]*
Alice: Have you been unplugging your sub-woofer?
[Himglish translation: Don't try placing the blame on me.]

I was sixteen, and dating my first boyfriend, when I first
became truly aware of the way money issues can throw a
spanner in the works of an otherwise jolly romance. In the
initial stages of our courtship, I was the major breadwinner
in the relationship, with takings of up to thirty dollars a
week from babysitting jobs. But then he got a job at
McDonald's, and just like that his income trumped mine.
On the occasions when we had our little adolescent spats,
my boyfriend was wont to point out (bless his little burger-
frying heart) that his more significant financial contributions
to our relationship meant that his opinion should carry
more weight. Though I would like to chalk up this issue
to the folly of youth, it has become apparent as the years
have rolled on that my high school sweetheart and I were

just being a wee bit precocious: financial imbalances are all too often at the root of tensions in relationships.

Financial conversations are almost always awkward, but making the weighty decision to move in with someone means that no matter how much you have managed to skirt around awkward discussions about money during the earliest phases of your courtship, it can no longer be avoided. No matter how much you and your partner are besotted with each other, discussing your finances is an activity that is, at best, tolerable. (I mean, I suppose it could be fun if your chat about money is your opportunity to declare 'I'm actually the fabulously wealthy scion of an ancient meat-tinning dynasty!' but I feel that is a less universal experience, and thus not one to be addressed here.) It is one thing to grapple with the intricacies (and adventures in passive aggression) that splitting costs with a flatmate with whom you are not sleeping can engender. But when you live with someone you love, discussions over payment of the council tax or who is going to take responsibility for keeping the household supply of recycling bags replenished can become charged in ways that can't always be simply diffused without them beginning to impinge in an often alarming fashion upon other areas of your partnership.

Unlike in generations past, it is quite safe to assume that when two people move in together they will both be in possession of sufficient income to support at least one person. Unfortunately, however, it is also quite likely that when two people move in together they will both be in possession of some debt – student loans, mortgages, too much fun with the credit card and overdraft – debt that, thanks to the global recession, is often waxing rather than waning.

Result? Figuring out how to manage a two-income household – regardless of whether you are married or just shacking up – has never been so delicate a matter. And although the epoch in which men were explicitly tasked with the responsibility of bringing home the bacon while women looked after cooking it is long gone, the fact remains that when it comes to finances, women are more likely to be at a disadvantage in contrast to their partners when they reach the point of cohabitation.

Now, when I began researching this section of the chapter, I demonstrated a serious (and uncharacteristic) lapse in judgement: I went into it assuming that women have, on average, more debt than men. We buy more shoes and handbags, right? And I am absolutely certain that I have read far more stories about credit-strapped ladies, illustrated with pictures of pretty girls looking sad while surrounded by those shoes and handbags, than about men who have been overly profligate with their spending on colourful vintage trainers and superfluous manbags.

But, though it rarely happens, I must admit that in this case, I was wrong. According to reliable research that was published in 2007, men in the UK are on average actually in twice as much debt as women, but women have a much harder time clearing their debts, in part because of the endurance of the substantial – on average, about 19 per cent – gender pay gap. In essence, we enter the workforce on a fairly even keel with men, but our salaries don't grow nearly as quickly, although our spending matches theirs – and, indeed, outstrips it in certain categories of consumption.

So what is the best way to establish a sense of financial equilibrium when the time comes for you to combine your households and it first becomes clear that all is not fair in love and your bank accounts?

First things first: you have to accept that a frank conversation about money has to come early, and pretty often, when you and your partner decide to move in together. Though it can feel like a major impediment to independence, if you are going to merge your domestic arrangements, it's essential to agree on a joint spending strategy. This might mean splitting everything 50/50, or it can mean pooling some of your income and keeping the rest separate. The former may make the person earning less money feel that he or she is getting a raw deal, but the latter can result in a rather tedious process of sorting and itemising receipts, using up time that you could spend on much nicer things to do as a couple, like having sex, or fighting over which set of parents you are going to spend Christmas with. While it is unlikely that you'll both entirely agree on the best way to manage money, it is desperately important that you communicate – clearly – what your views are on it so you don't end up with some nasty surprises (there's a reason that money issues are amongst the top reasons that couples of all generations split up).

To a great extent, it seems, in order to make living together work, it is important to be able to accept that what's yours is also your partner's, and vice versa – and that includes (awkwardly) any debt. Almost invariably, one of you is going to be on a higher income than the other (and statistically, that one is likely to be the man) and thus it just doesn't do to bring that disparity into the picture when you are squabbling, whether it is over something small – 'I make more money than you, so you should dust the picture frames' – or something rather larger – 'I paid off your massive student debt, so you are now beholden to me for ever.' It wasn't particularly nice when I was sixteen; it is quite inexcusable when you are any older. If you're not ready to share your assets – and it's perfectly fine if you're not – then maybe, just maybe, you should consider whether you're actually ready to share a home with someone whom you're not expecting to communicate with primarily via passive-aggressive Post-it notes written in florid Femalese.

Who do you fancy when you're at home?

As I mentioned earlier in this chapter, we're not only more relaxed (and enthused) about cohabiting with our romantic partners without worrying about the implications of dwelling in sin than previous generations; we're also far more keen to live with members of the opposite sex in totally platonic circumstances. Or, at least, ostensibly platonic circumstances.

Such households can be very beneficial indeed. Thanks to the apparently infinite magic of good old pheromones, of course, women who live together sometimes menstruate together, which means that everyone may be experiencing PMT symptoms simultaneously – that doesn't necessarily make for a happy home. And women's inclination to communicate indirectly (as we've discussed already) can often escalate into a battle of passive-aggressive leaving of notes that makes one's home a less-than-relaxed environment in which to dwell. Though we may do it with rather more politesse than our evolutionary predecessors, my consultant primatologist points out that lady monkeys who challenge the aegis of the alpha females in their dwelling groups tend to find themselves expelled, the monkey equivalent of being given notice by your flatmates that you'd better get cracking on Craigslist on finding a new place to live.

And while groups of men may be better at sorting out their differences in household maintenance styles: 'Dude, stop leaving the milk on the counter. It gets lumps' gets the job done rather more easily than a tangentially phrased message scrawled on the back of an envelope – the fact remains that when groups of men live together, it is not uncommon for a collective inclination to prioritise relaxation over tidiness to overcome them, perhaps in part due to a fear of gaining a reputation for being insufficiently masculine as a result of suggesting that they should engage in the stereotypically feminine activities of scrubbing and dusting (unless, of course, associated with military training, in which it's totally manful). Female flatmates will be less inclined to scoff – indeed, as I mentioned already, they may well be impressed by a man who can handle a sponge.

So it's agreed, then: in many cases, inter-gender platonic dwelling can be a lot more civilised, right? Right. Except, of course, when that crazy little thing called love – or at least attraction – rears its semi-inevitable, often-inconvenient, little head.

Why are we so intractably inclined to fancy our opposite-sex flatmates? There are two important reasons, I think. One is that even if we have grown up in non-traditional households, we have been socialised to expect that when men and women cohabit, they generally do so because they love each other, and therefore love should ensue from such an arrangement. Actually, this is a scenario in which the domisteric male has a particular advantage: if you are striving to seduce your female flatmate, a bit of showy housecleaning will probably go a long way to persuading her that you are someone a bit special.

The second reason, I do believe, is what I like to call the Ice-Dancing Factor (remember this important phrase, as it is something which will be rather importantly revisited later on in the chapter on men, women, and the workplace). Ice-dancers, of course, must spend a lot of time training very hard with their ice-dancing partners in order to be truly competitive at the sport. They eat, sleep and breathe ice-dancing and they do so side-by-side. So is it really surprising that in the (slightly uncommon) scenario in which both halves of an ice-dancing team are heterosexual, that they often end up having a romantic relationship? Nope.

And thus it is also not surprising that when two opposite-sex people find themselves cohabiting, it is not terribly unusual for one of them to start fancying the other. Alas, it is usually not the greatest love of all, so much as it is the love of greatest convenience: if the ultimate goal of romance is to find someone you love so much that you want to share your life with them, and you are already sharing your life with someone of the opposite sex, it might feel like you have done half the work already. For some people, this does lead to a lifetime of happiness together. But not always.

In fact, not that I want to be proscriptive, but I think that under such circumstances the only thing to do is for one of you to move out immediately. Only then can you possibly determine whether you are really falling for the person who platonically shares your home or whether, in fact, you are being rather unacceptably lazy. If moving out seems like too much of a hassle, then you can probably go ahead and tick the lazy box, and consider perhaps spending slightly fewer candlelit evenings at home drinking wine on the couch with your flatmate who is quite cute when you are lonely and you squint.

In summary . . .

Himglish: Old domestic rules are out. New domestic rules are in. Make dinner, but don't assume that it makes you into some kind of superhero.

Femalese: Counter to lingering expectations that many of us inherited from our mothers and grand-mothers, the domestic sphere is no longer as inherently feminised as it once was, bringing unprecedented aspects to the established chal-lenges of living in harmony with a male partner. Let him make you dinner, but make sure you get a turn with the crème brûlée torch.

6

Conflict: Sometimes, Men Are Jerks. Sometimes, Women Are Also Jerks

We are awfully hard on ourselves when we are in relationships that become problematic, that go from wonderful to good to bad to over. But if we are trying to embrace the concept of monogamy (and a majority of us are aiming for it) then we also have to accept the fact that failure is the most common outcome, and an outcome that occurs in very complicated ways. One of the few things that is clear about relationships, it is that in many cases when love, or something that seemed like it, falls to pieces, it is difficult to place blame, to determine whether the prince or the princess (or the frog) is ultimately at fault for turning your personal fairytale into a horror story. I am not saying that we should always set ourselves up to expect failure – we'd miss out on a lot of good things if that were the case (not to mention probably never leave the house, just to be safe from the perils of falling in love) but I do think that the first step in conquering conflict within relationships is to acknowledge upfront that the possibilities for dysfunction are manifold. Men cheat, women put excessive pressure on men to commit to things that they don't want, men don't communicate, women try to use communication to be unfairly manipulative. Except that in many cases, we've now come to realise, the actions of the respective parties can just as easily be reversed.

Swallow hard, because this chapter is not for the faint-hearted. But if you can make it through to the end (you are, of course, more than welcome to take breaks to give your eyes a little dab with a tissue here and there) it's my hope that this will give you some useful insights into the mysteries of what and how and why things can go wrong between men and women, when wrongness can be fixed or prevented through choosing to fight fairly, or not at all, and what to do in the difficult scenario when it becomes evident that the wrongness is so profound that you and your other half no longer make up something that even faintly resembles a whole.

You've got problems.

Alice:	Jonathan?
Jonathan:	Yes, dear?
Alice:	Why don't you buy me flowers anymore?
Jonathan:	I do buy you flowers. I bought you flowers, um, at some point not so very long ago. Last year, wasn't it?
Alice:	Don't you love me anymore? I am going to go and lock myself in the bathroom now and cry loudly. If you know what is good for you, you will bang on the door and beg me to forgive you.

If there is anyone out there reading this who currently feels exactly the same first flush of passion that you felt about your partner in the first week that you got together with him, please write me an email so that I can send you some kind of trophy through the post (I am, of course, only offering this prize to readers who have been with their partners for longer than a week). For the rest of you, please rest assured that the person who is getting the trophy is a giant freak and you are the normal ones. It is simply not possible for most couples to maintain exactly the same momentum and spark that they shared at the beginning of a relationship, if only because after a few weeks (or months, if you are still quite young) you realise that having sex all night, while great fun, is simply not as refreshing as a solid eight hours of sleep. And then you also recall that it is probably advisable for you to go to work once in a while rather than keep calling in sick so that you can carry on making hot, passionate love to your beloved. And at some point, you probably notice that he doesn't change his socks quite often enough or that she can be really rather contrary when it comes to selecting what the two of you should go to see at the cinema. So, yes, the honeymoon has got to end eventually for everyone, and because of this, the conclusion of it is not something to regard as a crisis. But often enough, that's exactly what we do.

Predictably, men and women tend to have different spins on what are the most telling signs that a relationship is entering a new, post-honeymoon phase. According to stereotype, men are centrally concerned by the fact that sex tapers off a bit – the forty-eight-hour sex marathons that often mark the initial stages of a relationship become less common, and panic ensues. For women, on the other hand, the end of the honeymoon period is often regarded to be marked by the gradual cessation of men doing the thoughtful, romantic things that they did in the first place to make themselves seem desirable – yes, just the things that make women feel more emotionally attached and valued by the men in their lives and therefore more inclined to have sex with them. Hello, vicious circle. And, like so many of the things that we've discussed already, it goes both ways: women find themselves wondering why they don't have much sex anymore, men begin to feel insecure because their other halves no longer make the kind of little, sweet gestures that once made them go gooey-eyed.

The trouble with this is that many of us are less inclined to acknowledge that this is quite a normal scenario, and much more inclined to take it that this kind of change in behavioural patterns is a sign that that we are no longer so much in love and doomed to fail. Then we get upset. We need to calm down, my dears.

Can we all agree, once and for all, that the honeymoon period is something that goes away but can also come back, and that we must stop thinking that it always has to be all or nothing? Unfortunately, because of our reluctance to persist with anything in the modern age, because everything can be replaced or improved upon as long as you throw a little bit of money at the problem, both men and women are inclined to scarper at the first sign of a slight lull. Mistake! A lull may be terrifying, but it is rarely a reason that you and your beloved should part. Don't expend your energy on worrying; by all means, make a conscious effort to bring back some of the things that you used to enjoy together when you first met (or perhaps introduce new things), or mention kindly to your beloved the things that he or she used to do which you loved, and now rather miss – without, of course, sounding like you are being all accusatory. Better, instead, to be kind, and deliver your small criticism through linking it to a positive experience.

Alice   You know, Jonathan, I always love it when you buy me flowers. Wouldn't you like to get me some more soon in order to make me happy? I think you would.

Jonathan: Uh, OK. I mean, I saw some half-price chrysantheums for sale in the garage forecourt earlier when I was buying some Lucozade. Shall I pop out and get some?

Alice: Well, that is not exactly what I had in mind, but I will be delighted to accept them in the spirit with which they are given.

It's rare, you see, that your partner has made a conscious decision to stop having sex with you or bring you presents; he is more likely to be feeling content and a little complacent and thus a little less inclined to push the boat out. This doesn't mean that he is being callous and doesn't love you. He's just, like most of the world, a bit lazy. And it is important to consider that he may be quite proficient at showing you love in ways that are a little less textbook and fairy tale, but actually probably mean a lot more because they are specific to your distinct relationship. Just because your boyfriend is not demonstrative in a manner that you expect, or even a manner in which you yourself would be demonstrative, doesn't mean that he is not very much in love with you.

Love takes lots of different forms over time, and thus sometimes, when you are feeling like you're in a little dip, you both should just accept that it needs to be ridden out: one day you will wake up, roll over to poke him because he has woken you with his snoring again, and be struck again by just how incredibly much you are in love with him. Yes, it takes a certain degree of endurance and dedication and stick-with-it-ness that is increasingly unfamiliar to us in our instant-gratification epoch, but I promise you, if you can get through that first slump, the next one will likely feel easier, because you will realise that your relationship does, in fact, have resilience. You'll find that you've acquired some of the kind of character that your mum was always urging you to build, and you and your other half can therefore look forward to sharing a long series of slumps and upswings. Romantic!

Clash of the Titans.

While everyone likes it when their romance is defined by smooth sailing, it is actually very healthy – and, I think, necessary – for you to have the occasional sparring match with your other half. The fact is that even the most simpatico couple is going to find themselves at an impasse now and then. While choosing to deal with minor disagreements through ignoring them, or simply ceding to whichever person has the more strident personality, may seem like a nice, easy solution, you can actually be doing yourselves a bit of a disservice if you let everything blow over in that fashion. While some couples like to brag that they never fight – and I've been half of several of them, because though I am pretty bolshy on paper I'm not very aggressive in person – and it all sounds rather lovely, those couples are also the ones who are more apt to break up because they run over a medium-sized bump in the road that, to them, seems to be impossible to surmount.

That's because sorting through the occasional bit of dissent over the placement of a wall hanging or whose family you should spend Christmas with gives your partner and you useful experience of going through the motions of disputing and reconciling. Though you may think that a spat over whether you should buy only organic vegetables may seem to have little in common with a major disagreement over whether both of you should up sticks and move to Abu Dhabi in order to pursue a job opportunity, working through those little differences means that when you find yourselves contending with a rather larger-scale difference you will be familiar with the way that each of you deals with conflict and – more importantly – confident of the way that you deal with conflict. You'll be secure in the knowledge that the two of you can fight and come out intact and in love as opposed to broken and dismayed.

But don't get me wrong: though arguing is inevitable, and I don't recommend sweeping stuff under the rug (unless it's dust, in which case, go on, be a slovenly housekeeper, I don't care), it is also advisable to ensure that you are not getting your conflict resolution practice through fighting over things that really don't need to be fought about at all. To whit: a lot of serious conflict arises between men and women about fairly non-serious things, because of our enduring habit of communicating about important issues in Himglish and Femalese. Remember how women express themselves more tangentially than men? Well, this style of communication is rarely so prevalent as when women are addressing something problematic or controversial: sometimes because we don't want to seem aggressive or bitchy, and sometimes because we are just damn tired of feeling like nags. But you know what? It is sadly not at all a good technique of working through a conflict, although it can be a great way to escalate one.

(Jonathan and Alice are discussing the upcoming weekend.)

Jonathan: My ex-girlfriend Pamela is in town. She suggested that she and I should meet somewhere for a quiet drink on Saturday night. She has something important to tell me. Is that OK with you?

Alice: I'm not your mother. I want you to do what you want.

Jonathan: OK, so I'll go out with Pamela then. You're sure you won't be lonely at home?

Alice: Whatever makes you happy.

(Alice remains aloof for much of the rest of the evening. Several hours later, Jonathan and Alice are getting ready for bed.)

Jonathan: Um, Alice? Is everything all right? You were really quiet at dinner. And then you threw your plate against the wall when you were finished.

Alice: You know what's wrong.

Jonathan: I do? Um, I don't, really.

Alice: GOD Jonathan, you are so insensitive!

Jonathan: You're so manipulative!

(Jonathan sleeps on the couch.)

Jonathan: The lads and I are going to the pub tonight. We're going to watch the game and we are going to be the lads! Pardon me while I beat my chest.

[Femalese interpretation: I'd rather spend my time with a bunch of drunken louts who I went to school with than with you.]

Alice: That's nice. I am going to have a quiet night in.

[Himglish translation: That is not nice. I will spend the evening sitting on the couch, watching reruns of an inspid sitcom about

annoying women living in New York, and definitely not have sex with you when you get home.]

Alice: Do you know what I want to do this Saturday?
           Go to IKEA and pick out some new slipcovers.
           Won't that be fun?

[Himglish translation: Hey! Let's have a really boring afternoon, which may or may not culminate with a plate of inexpensive, semi-delicious meatballs.]

Jonathan: Do we have to?

[Femalese interpretation: I possess the sophistication of a recalcitrant teenager. Why do you even bother going out with me?]

When women find ourselves and our boyfriends or husbands caught between a rock and a hard place, and we know what we want, we nonetheless often hesitate to express our opinion, instead asking the man in question what he thinks. We persuade ourselves that we do this because we are being considerate and interested in his opinion and don't wish to emasculate him by being a bossy shrew. But that's not really why we do it: at heart, we very often ask the men in our lives for their opinions on subjects on which we have already drawn undebateable conclusions, because we want them to demonstrate how sensitive and intelligent they are, and how in touch they are with our feelings, by giving us the answer that we would give if the same question were posed to us.

Are you really surprised by how infrequently this happens? I mean, really?

Oh, yes, occasionally it works, but so much more often it doesn't: to a Himglish-speaking man, when a woman says 'what do you want, dear?' it means 'whatever you want, dear' instead of, 'I want you to do what you know I want, but to pretend that it was your decision in order to reinforce my trust and confidence in your commitment to me and our relationship.' If we were really confident of his response, we probably wouldn't have bothered to ask him about it in the first place but would have just gone ahead and done it (which, you will note, is probably what he does when he genuinely thinks that you will unequivocally agree with him on something).

A big part of this problem comes down to emotional intelligence: just as women use language that is more suggestive than direct because they tend to be more adept at picking up on subtle meaning, so are we also more inclined to note subtle clues about the way that other people are feeling based on their body language, demeanour, facial expression or tone of voice. It's popularly referred to as a woman's 'sixth sense', but like many other things that seem to differ depending on gender, I suspect it comes down to a mixture of hardwiring (it's not coincidental that autistic spectrum disorders, which are symptomised in part by patients having difficulty relating to other people, are more often found in males) as well as a bit of socialisation. We tend to expect our daughters to be more sensitive than our sons, and thus raise them accordingly to take particular notice of the shades of other people's feelings, whether it's through giving them baby dolls to nurture when they are not much older than babies themselves, or holding them accountable for their kind treatment of the other kids in the playground while we excuse our sons for pounding the other kids into the tarmac because boys will be boys.

As a result, women tend to be quicker at reading men's moods than they are at picking up on ours – and we're also a bit more clever at knowing when they are lying or, for that matter, bracing themselves to break our hearts.

Conversely, we tend to get quite irritated when men do not respond to our similarly subtle signals – which, frankly, if you're already upset, is not really a good way to mitigate the situation. I find it much more useful to state when I'm in a mood rather than to wait for a few hours for a man to notice, which tends to stir me up into an undignified temper tantrum.

Not OK!:

Jonathan: How are you, Alice?
Alice: FINE.
[Himglish translation: NOT FINE.]
Jonathan: Oh good. I'm going to watch TV now.
Alice: You insensitive jerk!
[Himglish translation: You didn't notice how upset I am from my slumpy posture and tone of voice and now I feel even more sad and am unnecessarily redirecting my angst towards you.]

OK!:

Jonathan: How are you, Alice?
Alice: Actually, I am deeply grumpy. I have had a terrible day at work and I am also generally feeling dissatisfied with the state of the world. And, to be honest, I am not best pleased with the amount of time that you are spending at the office in the evenings when we could be having some quality time together.
Jonathan: I'm sorry to hear all that. Would you like a cuddle?
Alice: Yes, please.

See? Being straightforward works so much better. But I do have a lot of sympathy for those of my female readers who engage in what can be construed as passive-aggressive behaviour when they are upset, not least because I am sure that I, too, have often been guilty of it, and often have to make a conscious effort to act in an assertive way rather than the passive-aggressive one that comes naturally. As with so many other things that were drummed into our subconscious brains since birth, many women are convinced that we should avoid appearing angry or aggressive or outspoken at all costs – that it's unfeminine, not the sign of a so-called nice girl. Men, on the other hand, grow up being encouraged to say their piece, to stick their neck out, to be decisive, because such things are all associated with being masculine – which, it is important to note, isn't always easy for the guys out there who are inclined to be rather more retiring.

It's not exactly a win-win situation for girls: those of us who consider ourselves to be independent and feminist and regularly swan around inadvertently emasculating men still have to fight the urge, sometimes, to dial things down in order to avoid being all harridan-like. Unfortunately, of course, the result of all of this restraint is that we end up expressing our most heartfelt, angsty opinions in an indirect way and become passive-aggressive nags instead of plain old nags, which is hardly any better and will probably cause us more grief in the long run.

Still sceptical? Still depending on your partner to read your mind in order for you to feel like you are genuinely on the same playing field? Come on, girls: if you want trust and have confidence in your relationship, wouldn't it be quite good to start by setting an example: actually articulating your own thoughts rather than waiting for the man in your life to detect non-verbal cues that he has frequently proven himself to be unaware of? Yes, it would, and if the gentleman who the thoughts are being articulated to can't handle them then there is nothing wrong with thinking about finding one who can (or, at least, realising that you will simply have to train up the one you have on hand to listen). I hereby suggest that we all pledge to cut this kind of passive-aggressive fight-picking out of our relationship repertoires: not only will it reduce the number of spats that you have, it will mean that it is a heck of a lot easier for you to get to the heart of the matter when you and he are not seeing eye to eye, and move on more quickly to the make-up sex.

Your cheating heart

It is of course essential in any discussion of relations – and differences – between men and women, to bring up the nasty, but ubiquitous, c-word: cheating. But before we get properly into a rousing discussion of the difference between men and women when it comes to the commiting of – and being the victim of – infidelity, I am going to lay my unequivocal and quite judgmental opinion on the line: cheating is quite simply cruel and wrong. Yes, there are very complicated reasons why people cheat and why they justify cheating to themselves and why their partners forgive them for cheating, but ultimately if you are in a relationship with someone that has been defined as committed and you are dabbling in romance outside that relationship, then you are being quite unkind and you need to knock it off.

I don't care if your partner doesn't know about it, or if he does know about it and pretends not to care. I don't care if you feel it is justified because your ex-boyfriend cheated on you and you feel that it is your turn to get it out of your system, or because you have resigned yourself, after being the victim of a cheater, to the fact that everyone cheats. No! This kind of behaviour is mean and selfish and if you are telling yourself that it is better for you to stay in the relationship with your partner because he will be more hurt by your leaving him than by your cheating, or that he would cheat too if he had the opportunity, then you are kidding yourself. You know that you are kidding yourself. And I disapprove!

Because of this disapproval, if you admit to me that you are cheating on someone I will have no choice but to give you a loving, but stern, talking-to. And, in fact, I will also give you a very loving but stern talking-to if you have been party to cheating – that is, if you have been having a relationship, or even a mere dalliance, with someone, despite being aware of the fact that they are already committed to someone else. Both of these talkings-to will not only be about the fact that you are being horrible to someone else: they will also be about the fact that by cheating you are really being quite horrible to yourself.

In the first instance, you are letting yourself down by being an immoral cad; the guilt will only eat away at you and the knowledge that you are hurting someone you love (or think you love) will make you feel weak and pathetic, which tends to lead to a string of crap relationships. In the second instance, you are being horrible to yourself because you are allowing someone to put you in a position of disadvantage, of low value. Though you may believe in your heart of hearts that the person with whom you are having an affair loves you more than he does his 'official' partner, the fact is that the odds of being promoted from mistress to most special lady are only slightly higher than those of this book winning the Booker Prize. And furthermore, to paraphrase one famous twentieth-century

British roué, when a mistress becomes a wife, 'a vacancy is created'. People who cheat are likely to be repeat offenders, meaning that you'll end up spending you life looking for signs of your partner's unfaithful behaviours, with which you are all too familiar as a result of being his or her previous accomplice.

Now, very little of the content of my stern (but loving!) talk will actually be information that is new to you: with the exception of a few people who have some kind of pathological failure in the section of their brain that engages with morality, people who cheat know that it is unkind, horrible, and wrong, and must override a significant sense of self-loathing in order to carry on with it. But! We – and by we, I mean both men *and* women – carry on doing it anyway, with something like aplomb, if cruelty and unkindness can be executed with aplomb. Antiplomb? Yes, I think I shall call it that.

When it comes to displays of adulterous antiplomb, men have the worse reputation – perhaps because it has always been slightly easier for them to cheat, because in the most basic evolutionary sense they never get left holding the baby who doesn't resemble the person who they are committed to. Sometimes, in fact, they think that their membership in the cheatier sex is sufficient justification for their awful behaviour, like the man who explained his unfaithfulness to my feisty friend Bex by saying, 'I can't help the fact that I'm in love with two people.' ('Is one of them yourself?' she responded.) But just because it seems that men find it easier than women to separate sex and love doesn't mean that it means less when they cheat. 'I slept with her, but it was only physical,' remains a deeply cruel sentiment for a man to express to a woman to whom he professes to be committed, in an attempt to downplay the significance of an affair, since it is all too easy for a

woman to surmise from the expression of such a sentiment that her partner is utterly emotionally disconnected
from their own sexual relationship. Horrible.

In general, I think most people – both men and women
– know when they are cheating. Sure, you can prevaricate
all you want – 'it was only a few saucy text messages' or
'there was no penetration' or 'I didn't come' – but I'm
inclined to think that as soon as prevaricating feels like the
right thing to do, you should probably just be efficient and
move on to the part where you try to make amends, because
if you try to justify your antiplomb it's not because you
really have a legitimate excuse, it's because you know at
heart that you have done something wrong.

For many women, the prospect of falling in love with a
man with adulterous tendencies is a very frightening one.
Perhaps you are one of them; perhaps you spend time
thinking, 'Oh, if only I could identify ahead of time which
men were likely to be inclined to display a great deal of
antiplomb and cheat on me, then I could avoid them at all
costs, even if they are handsome and I am inexorably drawn
to them because of their resemblance to my father!' Well,
as it happens, over the last decade or so there have been a
number of studies done which have found that genetics
play a role in the likelihood that someone is going to cheat.
The most recent, a Swedish twin study that was published
in 2008, found that men who had a certain genetic 'flaw'
related to the uptake of a particular hormone in the brain
tended to be more likely to be unfaithful to, or have trouble
bonding with, their partners. Much buzzing ensued, of
course, thanks to some perfectly hilarious editors of a tabloid
newspaper who cheerfully dubbed it the 'love rat gene'.

But women are hardly innocent of this kind of naughty
behaviour either. We've already discussed quite a bit how
there has been a gradual evolution, especially over the last

fifty years, of the degree to which women need to depend upon being coupled up in order to attain social and economic stability. As the pressure for us to cleave to one man has decreased, it seems that we have become more interested in pushing our luck into the realms of experimentation outside the bounds of traditional commitments.

A 2006 American study found that lifetime infidelity rates for people over sixty was 28 per cent for men, up from 20 per cent in 1991, and 15 per cent for women, up from 5 per cent in 1991. And these studies were only measuring behaviour of people who were married, as opposed to people who cheat on their partners who they're in relationships with that have yet to be sanctioned by the state. And although we may not have that particular love rat gene, nature seems to come into play with women who cheat, as well. Another twin study found that women whose identical siblings cheated were more likely to step outside relationships themselves. And though it appears to go against our nature, whether due to genetics or the evolution of our sexual freedom, many women are perfectly capable of having physical relationships with men that lack an emotional component, although many are reluctant to admit this since it is still frequently regarded as a sign of lack of propriety.

It would be awfully helpful if this increased understanding of genetics was enough to prevent us from falling in love with philanderers, wouldn't it? But it isn't, of course: boys and girls, before you start bringing cotton swabs to cocktail lounges in order to gather DNA samples from the inside of the mouths of potential suitors and suitoresses before you will allow them to buy you a drink, it is important to keep in mind that while genes do exert a very strong influence on human development, they don't do so in a vacuum, and thus even a man who is carrying the love rat gene may be as faithful as your pet poodle, while a man who is devoid of it may only give love of the cheating kind. As the researchers were careful to point out, human behaviour is strongly influenced by social, cultural, and experiential factors in addition to genetic programming. People defy their genes all the time. For example, my genes dictate that I should have a thick monobrow. But I haven't sported one since I was about thirteen and discovered the wonders that could be wrought with a steady hand and a good, sharp pair of tweezers. While it is very interesting to know how behaviour and genetics are linked, ultimately it doesn't make for a very good excuse when you get caught with your pants down in the presence of someone other than the co-signatory on your joint bank account. With the exception, perhaps, of pathological behavioural or psycho-logical disorders (quite a different kettle of fish altogether, which you'll need more than a nifty book like this to contend with, I'm afraid) genetics doesn't deprive us of our free agency.

It is particularly interesting to note at this point, I do believe, how a side-effect of having the entire world at our fingertips courtesy of the Internet, has opened up a major new avenue for the would-be cheater. I like to call it in(ternet)fidelity. The trouble with in(ternet)fidelity is that in many cases the rhetoric and indeed the actual manifes-tation of the fantasy affair doesn't ever go beyond the kind of flirting that many happily coupled people have freely indulged in while at office cocktail parties for generations. The key difference, however, is that committing it to a screen, whether in the form of a Facebook message or an email or text, turns what might once have been a harm-less flirtation, a mild frisson, into a tangible act that can be quite easily witnessed by the other half of the once-happy couple.

Social networks make it particularly easy. Whereas the

act of asking a man or woman who is not your partner for his or her contact details so that you can flirt with them is basically clearly not on, Facebook and other social networking sites mean that people don't need any contact details besides a name and sometimes a face in order to find a way to start communicating with the object of their in(ternet)fidelous affection. Adding someone as a friend on Facebook is such a passive thing to do anyway – how many dozens of 'em do you have who don't mean anything to you? – that adding a really hot guy you might possibly want to sleep with, depending on the circumstances, doesn't seem like a huge deal. And sending that hot guy frisky messages is just once simple step further.

The fact may well be that the instigator of the in(ternet)fidelity genuinely doesn't take it seriously, doesn't regard it as anything beyond a bit of the kind of banter you have after three strong dry martinis with the prettiest lady at the marketing conference (or whomever). But seeing that kind of discourse written is rather more bruising to the person behind whose back the e-dalliance is going on. Furthermore, the sense of distance imposed on the communicator by the use of the computer means that quite often people will find themselves writing messages to men or women who they would never actually speak to in real life, much less speak to in a provocative or even affectionate manner.

Jonathan: Er, Alice, darling, I have a confession to make.

Alice: Yes, sweetheart? Did you forget to buy milk on your way home again?

Jonathan: Well, yes, I did. You see, I got waylaid because I was having sex with my secretary.

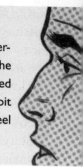

Alice: Excuse me?

Johnathan: I am so sorry, darling, but you must under-
            stand that it is not my fault, but rather the
            fault of my ancestors from whom I inherited
            the love rat gene. What bastards! Let's go spit
            on their graves, I'm sure it will make you feel
            much better.

Now, I realise as I write this rather excoriating condem-
nation of playing away, that you might be among the rather
substantial number of people who have cheated on their
partners. And if this is the case, you will probably be staring
at your shoes and feeling a bit awkward. But if the preceding
has made you retreat further and further into your jumper
with shame, don't worry, you cheating little cabbage: the
loving part of this ticking-off is still to come. For although
I disapprove so strongly of these kinds of steps being taken
outside the bounds of commitment, I am also aware that
people make these mistakes frequently, and that there is
a lot more grey in individual relationships than there is
black and white: just as different people have different
measures of commitment, they will also have different ideas
of what constitutes cheating.

For example, it is a widely held belief that men consider
sexual infidelity to be more serious than women do, while
women find the idea of their partner being emotionally
intimate with another woman more troubling and less easy
to forgive if he was just having anonymous sex with another
woman. And sometimes the prospect of losing a partner
is worse than staying with one who is not faithful. While
I believe you may have to accept that it is pretty unrea-
sonable for you to expect to get forgiveness from your

original partner unless he or she is of an especially saintly nature, I also don't think that anyone should be branded with a scarlet letter 'A' and deprived of the opportunity to be forgiven or, if forgiveness is impossible, not be allowed to love again.

But that doesn't mean that you are completely off the hook, by any means. I do expect that you will take responsibility for your actions. Yes, it is true that both male and female philanderers may be influenced by more than just an inclination to be naughty. It is not possible to definitely say whether it's because they are driven to it by their genes or their upbringing or if it just becomes easier with practice, which is to say that once you have violated the taboo of fidelity once it simply becomes more easy to violate, less taboo-ish – kind of like when you first started having sex. I suspect that while the adage 'once a cheater, always a cheater' may well be true, it may have as much to do with the cheater's own lack of self-respect that he continues to cheat after getting caught, as much as the fact that he is driven to it by some fluke of evolution. That's quite sad. So if you agree to strive to attain some self-awareness and really think about why you chose to step beyond the bounds of propriety in your relationship, than I agree that you should be absolved of your transgressions and permitted to have a second chance at love.

In other words, in order for you to regain your nice-person stripes, you need to have a think about why you cheated, and you need to think about it while keeping in mind that the answer is never, 'he drove me to it' (unless he gave you a lift down the road to meet your illicit lover). As with other damaging behaviour, people cheat for a wide variety of reasons which are not always tied to dissatisfaction with their relationships so much as they are dissatisfied with themselves, although it also seems that we increasingly cheat in order to create a reason to end a relationship that already has something deeply wrong with it that can't be fixed, but which is not very tangible and difficult to articulate.

Somehow, both men and women often find that it feels easier to say 'it's over, because I am having an affair' than 'it's over, because I don't really love you any more and sometimes just listening to you breathe through your nose at night makes me feel a little bit suicidal and also I am not sure that I can grow old with someone who holds your particular views on graduated tax brackets', simply because the former is a simple and unequivocal reason you have to leave. It can allow you to avoid the actual process of grappling with the true complexities of your feelings yourself, much less making you explain them to someone who speaks the mystifying language of the opposite sex. It is also, of course, selfish, lazy, and unkind, and therefore will always be another thing that is quite unacceptable.

But if you have been on the receiving end of this kind of unacceptable behaviour, I think it is also very important for you to prevent it from defining your relationships in the future. Almost as bad as being cheated on is the development of an intractable fear of being cheated on: assuming that your next partner will do it simply because your previous one did is a great way to poison an otherwise lovely relationship, since few people take kindly to having their text messages and emails snooped through even if they are perfectly innocent. If you feel like a previous bad experience has filled you with a sense of permanent fear, then I suggest you work on overcoming that before you consider moving into a new relationship.

It's you. It just is.

Maisie: Alice, [sobs] Toby and I broke up.

Alice: Oh, Maisie. I'm so sorry. I shall be over in a few minutes with several pints of ice cream, because nothing will make you feel better about the devastation of your love affair quite like the distraction of a crippling stomachache.

Maisie: But Alice! I'm lactose intolerant.

Alice: Even better.

Few things are quite so devastating as break-ups. Most adults are used to dealing with a bit of disappointment, maybe even a touch of tragedy, in the course of our lives, but somehow the experience of being rejected by the person you love (or thought you loved) never seems to get any easier from the first time it happened when you were a teenager.

Personally, after years of experience and my own fair share of defunct relationships, I have developed a method for dealing with a terminated romance that involves taking to my bed like a consumptive heroine in a nineteenth-century novel. I then languish there until I get over the relationship or I get bored, depending on which happens first (it is usually the latter). Of course, at that point I often don't really feel very much better, but at least I've accepted that I have to get on with my life, which is sometimes all that one can do under these extreme circumstances.

And in these circumstances, I at least feel quite lucky that I'm female – whereas we seem to expect women, fragile and emotional creatures that we are, to go through these grieving periods, men don't get nearly as much sympathy. Whereas it would almost seem unnatural for me not to spent the first days post-break-up languishing, crying, eating too much, and eventually spending hours going over the post-mortem of the relationship with my girlfriends, the enduring expectations that men should be tough and strong means that they often end up doing their crying in secret.

Toby: Maisie and I broke up. She realised that she doesn't love me enough to be with me for the rest of her life and it has really thrust me into a state of existential crisis. I don't know who I am without her. I don't think I will ever find any woman to love again and I also am beginning to wonder if it really is because I am a bit fat.

Jonathan: Uh, that sucks, man. Do you want another pint? Maybe you will feel better if you pull that girl over there. I feel uncomfortable.

I suspect all of that secretiveness can feel a bit poisonous and horrible after a while. In fact, because of that suspicion, even in the cases where I have split up with men at their behest and I am arguably the injured party, I always find myself worrying after a few days that they might be suffering more than me because they have no one to offer them adequate consolation. (This attitude is, of course, at least a touch patronising, but hey! It makes me feel better.)

The end of a relationship is often so messy and awful and complicated that it can be even more difficult than usual to unpick the role that gender plays in influencing our behaviour. In the interest of research, I decided to send a little survey around my friends to find out what their experiences had been and was not a little bit amused when, within a short period of time, my friend Ella remarked, 'Why don't men understand that when I don't call them, it means I'm not interested?' while my friend Anna wrote, 'Why do men think that not calling is an acceptable way to convey a lack of interest?' Hm. So women are allowed to stop calling but men are not? How confusing. This obviously requires quite a bit of reflection.

As we've discussed throughout this weighty tome, the fact that we are inclined to become sexually intimate before we become emotionally intimate with people who we are dating causes an acceleration in relationships that can prove to create a wide range of particularly awkward scenarios when the time has come for them to end. On the one hand, for example, there is the one-night-stand, which is often concluded by one of the parties refusing to acknowledge the other one ever again – a particularly humiliating experience for the unacknowledged person. And then there is the third-date break-up: if you haven't slept with someone, it should be perfectly fine after only three meetings to send an apologetic email and avoid a dramatic and woeful scene, but somehow when you've known someone biblically a few times both men and women often find themselves feeling like they need to let the unwanted person down properly and easily, which is quite awkward to be on the receiving end of from someone whose middle name you don't know (or particularly care to know).

Perhaps the most significant difference between men and women when it comes to the end of relationships is that they tend to behave somewhat in opposition to the manner in which they do in other aspects of the relation-ship. Men tend to take a more passive approach, because they are so terrified of the fury of a woman scorned, while women choose to be more assertive because they wish to wrest as much control of the situation as possible. I think this is likely because as much as they may view us as equals, men continue to feel a certain onus to be gentlemanly; unfortunately, modern interpretations of gentlemanliness tend to be rather heavily focused on not causing a woman visible upset.

Thus, many modern men opt for the no-contact technique that my friend Anna complained about, perhaps hoping that if they spend enough time ignoring their soon-to-be-erstwhile lady friend that she will get the message or, in the best-case scenario, assume that he has died in the course of committing some sort of selfless act, therefore rendering him incapable of breaking her heart. And, of course, this also absolves him of the problem of having to articulate his feelings – something that he may be less well equipped for as a result of his lower word ration, in addition to the wider cultural reluctance for men to be very emotional.

Of course, for the modern crème brûlée-torching man, being in touch with feelings is considered something of an accomplishment. Unfortunately, however, this doesn't make the fact that you are breaking up with someone much better: when one ex-suitor of mine looked at my tear-streaked face and said, 'Well, at least I didn't do this by text message' I wasn't exactly inclined to thank him for his incredible consideration of my feelings, but in retrospect, his approach was far superior to many: one girl I know was dumped via a note left tucked under her wind-shield wiper by her boyfriend, while another was devastated when her boyfriend simply left the country – he told her he was going on vacation, but it soon became apparent that actually, he was never coming back.

But in the interest of showing how twenty-first-century they are, some men, sensitive to the rampant stereotyping of their callousness, really take it to the other extreme: they're so focused on being respectful and considerate that they go through the motions of breaking up with a woman they've only seen briefly as if they've been together for years, which can be humiliating in its own special way. I once had nothing more than dinner on two occasions with a man before he walked me home, stood outside my block of flats, welled up, told me that he couldn't go on with our relationship and begged me to be his friend. I went upstairs and took to my bed in best consumptive-heroine style for ten minutes until I remembered that, although I had just been through the motions of a major break-up, I actually hadn't been in a relationship.

The moral of all these stories? Boys, you can't really make dumping any nicer than it is, so please just try to make it as direct as possible, like yanking off a plaster: kidding yourself that it is kinder to a woman to be evasive and vague is really just a way of being selfish by trying to avoid as much of the fall-out as possible, but going to the other extreme of assuming that you are ruining her life is not necessarily the kindest approach either. Do it in person, but do it in proportion to the amount of time you've actually spent together.

But before you think that I am being too hard on my Y-chromosomed friends, please realise that I fully acknowledge that while we get less of a bad rap, women are not really very much better at ending relationships in ways that are minimally messy. In contrast to the male approach, we tend to go for something rather more complicated, in keeping with our general pursuit of obfuscating our communications. Thus, instead of merely being able to say, 'I'm sorry,' we employ the adept right sides of our brains to create complicated narratives to justify the vagaries of our hearts. We also do it to give ourselves the confidence – for, after all, we will often be externally perceived as the one who loses out the most, simply by being rendered single – that we are in control. Result? Too often, this approach leads to a break-up that is incredibly protracted and results in the unnecessary attrition of both parties.

Several of my dearest friends, for example, swear by a technique of ending things with men they have been dating semi-seriously by meeting them for coffee and saying, 'I feel like you think that we would be better as friends.' This is, of course, a clever attempt to hijack the male mind: they know that the fellows in question will interpret this classic Femalese statement literally and therefore conclude that they have been sending out platonic signals and have thus essentially instigated the break-up themselves. Unfortunately, sometimes the men think that these women really do want to be friends with them, which is rarely the case. This can lead to a series of intense, heart-to-heart conversations over too many lattes that fail to get to the true heart of the matter: it's over. I don't really think that this, or other similarly complicated narrative approaches, is really any better than the male no-contact option: women who employ this technique are still attempting to absolve themselves of responsibility.

The trouble with this, of course, is that whether you are a boy or a girl, when you absolve yourself of responsibility for the failure of a relationship in these rather manipulative fashions, no matter how many times you say, 'It's not you,' and mean exactly that (because you speak Himglish) or actually are trying to imply something else (because you speak Femalese) the person who you are attempting to let down easy will come to the conclusion that they are in fact at fault. Which is something you most likely already know to be true, because you have most likely been in that situation yourself.

And frankly, if you are the one making an effort to reclaim your freedom, the least you can do it shoulder the responsibility for hurting someone's feelings rather than trying to make them think that you're the hurt party. It's simply the only grown-up option. And if you are not willing to take the grown-up option in these unavoidably unhappy set pieces, if you are not capable of doing unto others as you would have them do to you, then maybe you should consider revisiting your primary school education? It's not rocket science.

But before we close this chapter on a sulky note, let me point out that there is a bright side to all of this: break-ups are awful, but you know what is much worse? Being in a bad relationship! And now that we live in an era where we are more free than ever to control our romantic destinies, we have the chance to escape souring relationships of the sort that might once have been tantamount to being sentenced to a lifetime of suffering and find sweeter ones. So take comfort in that next time you're dumped. I mean, you'll still cry, and that's fine, but perhaps it might encourage you to make your consumptive heroine stage a wee bit briefer.

In summary . . .

Himglish: Don't go breakin' my heart.

Femalese: I won't go breakin' your heart. Well, I might, to be honest, because the majority of relationships end in heartbreak. But I shall try to eschew doing it in an excessively cruel way because I am keenly aware that I should strive to treat others as I'd like them to treat me: with kindness, respect, and sympathy.

7

The Office: Men, Women, Professional Conduct . . . and the Stationery Cupboard

I was young and innocent and barely employable. Working on the reception desk of a film company, I had big dreams, limited skills (trying to answer the telephone, I actually managed to break the handset) and a very tedious remit that involved sorting the post, buzzing people through the front door, and summoning couriers to drive video tapes around the city. Are you really surprised that I started fancying the gangly young chap who walked back and forth past the reception desk every day, schlepping coffees and toast to the producers? No, of course you are not.

And are you really surprised that when I ended up going out for drinks with my temporary colleagues that Friday night I got quite drunk and kissed the toast-schlepper while all of them were watching? And – hold on to your chairs, now – are you shocked and appalled that on Monday I felt so profoundly embarrassed by my uncharacteristic and shameful behaviour that, even though I was only due to work there for one more week, I could barely drag myself into the office? That we became figures of fun for the entire company, and that he never really spoke to me again, for fear of compromising his ambitions of getting promoted to handling the producer's bagels? No, no, and no. It is the oldest story in the book when it comes to work relationships – but it is a story that only begins to scratch the surface of the challenges that arise when men and women interact in the office.

In an ideal world, one's workplace (unless one works in the sex industry, perhaps) should be a place where one's gender should be less of a factor than it is anywhere else, shouldn't it? It should. Stop laughing! No really, stop. OK, you're right to laugh, in a way, because the only reasonable alternative, really, is to cry, since even I cannot see the hilarious side of a lot of what goes on in our boardrooms and typing pools. The fact is that many workplaces remain key battlegrounds in the war between the sexes, if you are combative and like to call it that – having rather dovish inclinations, I would prefer to think of it as a journey to understanding between the sexes. Whatever you call it, however, the attainment of that understanding still seems – quite worryingly – very far away, even though I think that we have lived in an ostensibly post-feminist world long enough that it is simply ridiculous for anyone to admit that the concept of a gender-neutral workplace is not just something for the PC brigade to strive towards. It just makes good sense for women, for men, and for the men and women who employ them. Right? Right.

But despite the fact of this obvious good sense, and the well-meaning and sometimes extensive efforts that many of us have made to level the playing field for the sexes in professional contexts, the working world remains one of the areas of our lives where sex comes into play more than any other. This is the case whether you are using the word 'sex' to describe an individual's biological gender, or you are actually employing the word to refer to the act of love (or, perhaps more accurately, the act of lust) which, according to tradition, must be manifested in stationery cupboards when two people who have spent a lot of time peering at each other from behind the shelter of their computer monitors have had a little bit too much fun at the annual Christmas party.

And thus, in this chapter I shall take a two-pronged approach to looking at how we work together. First, we'll consider whether men and women's strengths and weaknesses as thinkers and doers are determined by their sex, and how these apparent strengths and weaknesses affect the way that we work together. That part will be sensible and interesting and elucidating. Then we will take a look at the more social side of office life, and how gender comes into play there – it will be much less sensible but, just as office gossip often proves to be a greater incentive to go in to the office than the actual work that you will be doing there, much more interesting.

Anything you can do, I can do better.

Men and women are a competitive lot, aren't we? The seeds of it are planted on our primary school playgrounds when we are just big enough to differentiate between boys and girls. We decide that we don't like each other because we are not of the same sex, and although we outgrow that before too long and start, for the most part, liking each other far too much, a substantial degree of that sense of competitive edge between the sexes is maintained into adulthood and carried in to the workplace.

Women have been integrated into the workforce on a large scale since the Second World War (six decades, that's certainly not to be sneezed at), and now those who choose to be stay-at-home-mothers or housewives are something of a bizarre exception rather than a rule. In fact, it is exceptional to the extent that some young women are choosing to pursue the mimicry of 1950's house-wifery (which has little in common with the challenging realities of the life of the contemporary stay-at-home women) as their life's work because it seems so deliciously subversive and even a little bit kinky to dedicate their lives to wearing pinnys and baking cakes while waiting patiently for their husbands to come home. And even those of us who have long since given up on making cakes because of our propensity to burn the pans may occasionally find ourselves having a little bit of an emotional wobble where we wonder if our lives wouldn't be easier if we just set out to marry a nice billionaire and spend the rest of our lives shopping and ensuring that we maintain the façade that we are never any older than twenty-nine. (Easier, perhaps; hideous and dull and intolerable, indubitably.)

But despite the fact that housewifery is increasingly a fringe activity, a certain tension about the presence of both men and women at work has shown a remarkable endurance. And I, for one, think this enduring tension is still grounded, after all these years of advancement, in a strange, antiquated sensibility. You see, despite our massive inroads into many professions that were once dominated by men (medicine being a particularly notable one, with female medical students in the UK and the US now outnumbering male ones) few women over the course of their careers do not find themselves entangled in a scenario where their sex is considered by someone to potentially compromise their fitness for work. This may be because they are thought not to possess the physical strength for a job or because they might possibly want to take maternity leave at some point. Facing this kind of challenge is something that few men can relate to first-hand, and thus creates what can sometimes seem like one of the most unbridgeable gaps between the sexes.

We are, happily, long past the point where any reasonable person still argues that men are intrinsically more intelligent than women – neuroscientists have proven several times over that we are all born with essentially the same baseline of cognitive abilities. However, over the course of our young lives these will invariably be affected – by environment, by the kind of education we receive, and, in many cases, by cultural expectations of what sort of thinking that people of our gender should be good at.

There are very good reasons that people are not allowed to discriminate between potential employees on the basis of their gender. But this is not to say that there are not also some interesting differences in the way which men and women tend to think and behave, which I believe may cast some light on why working with colleagues of the opposite sex can somewhat be frustrating and confusing – but also why there are some scenarios where having both a man and a woman on the job might lead to the most fruitful kind of professional collaboration.

Approaches to work

'Alice,' said her boss, Richard, on a busy Tuesday afternoon, 'what are you doing? You look busy, but I actually have no idea what you are up to.'

'Oh,' said Alice. 'Nothing much. I'm checking my voicemails, writing an email to that client in Dubai and having a conversation over instant messenger with Fred in accounts about next week's payment run. Is there something else that you'd like me to take care of?'

'Er,' said Richard. 'Well, would you mind terribly taking this jacket to the drycleaner?'

'Of course not,' said Alice. 'Why else do you think I spent all that money on my postgraduate degree? I can take that three o'clock conference call on my mobile while I'm on my way there.'

'Jonathan,' said his boss, Penelope, 'can I have you take a look at this presentation?'
'Sure,' said Jonathan, 'as soon as I finish calculating my expenses.'
'Of course,' said Penelope. 'Don't panic. One thing at a time.'

When we were growing up, my older brother used to always yell at me for having a short attention span because of my failure to pay careful attention when he wanted me to watch him playing computer games (which is in itself a common male request that I will never be able to understand). It was not that I was refusing to sit next to him while he struggled to reach the next level of *Prince of Persia*; it was just that I preferred to also be reading a book or knitting a sweater for my favourite stuffed bunny rabbit while he did it. One passive activity was simply not enough stimulation for my brain.

Having been deeply stigmatised (sniffle) by that older brother harassment (he may never have gotten over my mockery of his wild curly hair, however, so I guess that we're even), I lived for many years with the belief that I had an inadequate attention span. But then I discovered the concept of multi-tasking – something, of course, that I had been doing my whole life. Doing lots of things at once, I was delighted to learn, is not just considered to be a perfectly legitimate way of going about your business, but it is something that, on average, women excel at, whilst men somewhat lag behind.

Of course, generations of women could have told you this, having rolled their eyes to heaven a million times as a result of husbands and boyfriends who appeared to be incapable of being vested with responsibility for more than one errand at a time. But neuroscientists have confirmed it: a number of studies indicate that while men and women may initially appear to be equally good at multitasking, the results produced show that women tend to be more effective and accurate when they're carrying out more than one task simultaneously.

There may be physiological reasons for this – the section of the brain that joins the right and left halves, which is called the *corpus callosum* (remember that for your next stint on *University Challenge*), is thicker in women, which apparently indicates that it is easier for us to use different sections of our brains simultaneously. Furthermore, other research has pointed to women's proficiency in multi-tasking as having an obvious evolutionary function. We may have developed this behavioural trait because, at the most basic level, of the extent to which women looking after children must contend with competing demands on their attention, especially when there is more than one child in the home – skills which have now been applied to the project of being able to speak on the phone, answer emails and do filing simultaneously while our male colleagues look on in disbelief.

I can't tell you how many times I have been accused by men of not listening to them talk because I have been busy doing something else, only for me to be able to rattle off their last five sentences word for word. Of course, this usually makes them feel more, rather than less, annoyed, so now I try to humour them by pretending when they speak that I am only listening to them. But you can be sure that even when I do that I am also making mental shopping lists and considering solutions to the global energy crisis. In an age when we are all being bombarded by a constant influx of information that comes from several directions at once, it is great to be a natural multi-tasker, and it helps women stand out in jobs where juggling more than one project or client or problem at the same time is essential – which, these days, is pretty much any job.

But before you start feeling incompetent, boys, please be aware that I am not suggesting that you don't have anything unique to bring to the table yourselves. Far from it! On average, compared to women, men tend to be better at seeing the so-called bottom line: that is, while their female colleagues may be better at thinking laterally, men tend to be more task-focused and process-oriented. They are focused not just on outcomes, but on how things work – and are thus inclined to develop what is known as expert knowledge. Directed in the right way, this approach to work can be extremely effective and useful; misdirected, of course, it can lead to men spending a bit too much time cataloguing their record collections.

But what use is all of this? Well, every job requires problem-solving to some degree, but few problems – with the exception, perhaps, of some of the questions on your algebra homework – can only be solved through one technique or intellectual approach. Thus, the real value in having some understanding of how men and women might approach problems differently is not to prompt gender discrimination (that only leads to awkward and expensive employment tribunals, people) but rather to help us all understand that just because we would tackle an issue differently from our opposite-sex colleagues doesn't mean that they are doing it wrong. But it may well be indicative of the way that our brains and our inherited behaviours can be quite different. And, of course, it is important to note that just because one style of thinking doesn't come most easily to you because of your gender, multi-tasking is not like pregnancy: men can learn to do it too, just as women can train themselves to narrow their focus when necessary.

Hopefully, the generation that has entered the workplace within the last five years or so will mature into pioneers of an even more equitable workforce, but the fact that some of my own contemporaries continue to conduct business meetings in strip clubs and cede to the pressure to trade career advancement for sexual favours doesn't fill me with absolute confidence. But I am optimistic that if those of us who avoid these kinds of approaches to the working world stay strong, we will get there in the end.

Management

Considering the contrasts in male and female management style is a bit of a delicate issue, to say the very least. It is impossible to overlook the fact that women in management positions are, in many fields, worryingly exceptional. Some people would argue that the relative dearth of women in management positions is due to the fact that they are not as good at being in charge; I would argue that those people are idiots, and I would win the argument.

In fact, most vaguely enlightened thinkers acknowledge that a long history of discrimination against women in the workplace – whether of the direct, odious kind or the more tangential but deeply challenging sort in which businesses and organisations are inflexible when it comes to accommodating employees who also have family responsibilities – is more at fault, rather than some kind of intrinsic, ineffable, female inability to oversee things.

Researchers have established that there are interesting trends in the differences between the ways that men and women approach management. Men in leadership roles tend to be more self-centred: their management strategies tend to have an underlying goal of personal attainment of higher status (or higher pay, or other forms of professional advancement) with less focus on the well-being of the people who are being managed. Not surprisingly, this trait can also be seen in men who are in sub-management positions: they tend to be more competitive with their colleagues and more goal-oriented than women.

Women, on the other hand, tend to show a greater affinity for focusing on looking after the development of those they are managing, and the company overall, in addition to their own careers. Men are associated with so-called 'hard' skills – being aggressive, single-minded, and keeping focused on the bottom line, while women are expected to display 'soft' skills – sympathy, intuition, and the ability to listen with care and due consideration to colleagues (yes, it's that mythical 'sixth sense' at work again). Women are celebrated for their proficiencies at cooperation in circumstances where men are lauded for their thirst for competition.

And how does this play out in the workplace? Women may often be regarded as less ambitious than their male counterparts, which may mean that they don't get promoted as quickly – even though this so-called feminine approach to management may be better for the company as a whole. As demonstrated with great piquancy in the 2008 US presidential election by the reaction to the candidacy of Hillary Clinton, women who do show a lot of ambition, and perhaps take a more stereotypically 'male' approach to their work, are almost invariably labelled as bitches or ball-breakers or other things that are even more offensive.

One 2007 American university study tested managers' ability to detect emotion in facial expressions and vocal tones, and then asked their staff to rate their managers' sensitivity to emotions and the level of satisfaction the staff had with the management. Result? You probably won't be entirely surprised that the staff members had higher opinions of male managers with low sensitivity to emotions than of female managers who weren't very intuitive. Furthermore, another study from the same year that was referenced in the *Harvard Business Review* (so you know it is serious) found that the most successful CEOs in the US are those with the so-called hard skills rather than the soft ones, which doesn't exactly work in women's favour either when there is so much pressure on us to demonstrate our proficiency at being soft.

And then, on top of all these intangible pressures for women to conform, there is the issue of physical appearance. If you have always assumed that women who are more attractive are more likely to be employed, you would be right: data in numerous studies has backed that up. While men have their own physical issues to deal with – those who are of average height or below have a harder time getting jobs and getting ahead in their careers when they are competing with beanpoles – the overall focus on women's appearances tends to be more sustained, whether it is because they are showing too much flesh, as British Home Secretary Jacqui Smith was criticised for after being filmed in a V-neck top by an elevated camera in the House of Commons, or not showing enough, as was the case with one young woman in London in 2007 who was told that she could not have a job as a hairdresser because she wore a headscarf.

Quite often, these kinds of biases are incorporated company-wide: for example, one large London City firm felt it was necessary to draft in image consultants to advise its female employees on appropriate dress for the workplace. Dress codes are one thing, but scrutinising the appearance of professional women to that extent invariably objectifies us in a way that our suited and booted male colleagues are not and which, I believe, often causes some confusion when male colleagues do not understand, or become patronising about, what they perceive to be female colleagues' excessive attention to the way that they look.

It's all really very disheartening for those of us women who maintain some ambition to do things with our lives other than marry well. Fortunately, evolution in some corporate cultures over the last decade or so points to increased recognition that the alpha-male style of working is not necessarily a superior one. It makes me feel a little less disheartened when I note that more progressive public- and private-sector organisations are increasingly including mandates for equality in their human resource policies. But there is still a long way to go: women still fail to receive equal pay for equal work. With women receiving 17.5 per cent less than their male colleagues in the UK (in 2007) for full-time work, and leaving management positions with far higher frequency than men, it clearly remains far harder than it should be for women to attain equity in the world of work.

It's business time.

Right, now that we have gotten the serious side of gender in the workplace out of the way – admit it, it was totally elucidating and fascinating, wasn't it? – we can address when sex in that other sense crops up in the office. Sex should be kept out of the workplace at all costs, of course. But also, of course, there are few offices that aren't rife with it in one form or another along the spectrum of possible office sexuality – whether it is due to the ever-present scourge of sexual harassment, the unique modern phenomenon of the office marriage, or simply engagement in full-blown office affairs.

Alice's new boss, Malcolm, asked her to meet him for a drink to discuss her newest project proposal.

'Meet me at my club,' Malcolm said to her, 'at half nine.'

Half nine seemed a rather late hour to discuss a project proposal, but Alice knew that Malcolm was busy.

He was halfway through a large glass of white when she arrived.

'Alice,' he said, smiling, 'do sit down. What can I get you to drink?'

'Oh,' she said. 'I'm fine. I'm really excited to talk about the new project.'

'Oh, right,' said Malcolm, raising his eyebrows. 'I haven't actually looked at that yet. Oops! More wine, darling?'

'But if you haven't looked at it yet . . .' Alice began to say, but stopped herself. If they weren't there to discuss work, she realised, and because they certainly weren't friends, it would appear that Malcolm had tricked her into going on a date.

Under the table, she texted Jonathan: Pls ring in fifteen minutes and shout into phone about flat being on fire. Thanks. xxx.

In the 2008 film *How To Lose Friends And Alienate People*, there's a scene where the protagonist, Sidney, a bumbly Englishman played by the adorable Simon Pegg, is confronted by his boss, Lawrence – older, suaver, American – about his behaviour towards women in the office.

'When I do it, it's flirtation,' says Lawrence about Sidney's flair for lechery. 'When you do it, it's sexual harassment.'

Everyone is more relaxed these days about the rules of propriety between men and women, and as you will have figured out already, I am generally in favour of this. But sometimes we do still have to adhere to some rules. Usually I don't look to the cinema to tell me the meaning of life, but in this case I do believe the scriptwriters were spot on in identifying one of the greatest challenges to men and women who work together: determining the difference between the kind of jolly flirting that can make the time at work pass quicker and the sort of sinister harassment that can ruin lives. Because of the enduring and widespread belief that people (and the people are usually women, for non-mysterious reasons) who complain about harassment are making mountains out of a little bit of sexy joshing and being overly politically correct, many victims of this kind of treatment feel that they have no choice but to go on enduring it rather than facing the wringer that the complaints process – if one even exists – involves. So we frown, or even giggle anxiously, because we feel powerless to make a fuss, and the perpetrators of the harassment assume that we must be enjoying it.

But of course we are not enjoying it at all: ultimately, the reaction of the person on the receiving end of the attention determines whether it is harrassment. There will always be things that you can say to one colleague that another will find deeply offensive; that's where you have to use your discretion and sensitivity. The crux of the problem in these situations, I believe, is a combination of women failing to speak up for themselves because they are afraid of being regarded as whingers, or even of losing their jobs – and indeed, in many cases, failing to speak up for each other when they witness that kind of harassment going on, because they too are intimidated by the atmosphere that it creates – and of men being oblivious (or choosing to be oblivious) when their behaviour crosses the line. It's rubbish, and we all need to work harder to make sure it stops.

Girls, if someone is making you uncomfortable, tell him

to knock it the hell off and don't let him intimidate you: just because someone else might enjoy working in an office environment that is tantamount to that in a *Carry On* film doesn't mean that you have to cede to it.

Boys: if you are inclined to engage in something which you believe is just a bit of flirtation because, gosh, that girl who sits across from you wears pretty short skirts, please, for the love of all that is good and right, take a moment to consider her reaction. If she doesn't laugh, or only laughs awkwardly; if she looks like you would if your football team just lost; if she stops making direct eye contact with you (something I once did for three months after the colleague who sat next to me wouldn't stop talking about his sexual conquests in lurid detail every Monday morning) – well, then you should consider the possibility that you may have overstepped the bounds of propriety.

And everyone? Regardless of your sex, there is no reason for you to hesitate to intervene if you witness someone being treated in a way that is demeaning. You don't need to make a giant fuss – just a quick word (or an email) will often make a huge difference and make the victim feel, well, less victimised. The worst incident of sexual harassment that I ever experienced was made so much worse by the fact that after it happened, all of my colleagues – women and men – laughed. That really wasn't good at all. There are so many things in life that are hilarious: perhaps we should make a collective effort to focus on another one of them being the focus of fun in the office.

Until five o'clock do us part.

It was Wednesday afternoon, and Jonathan was at work, manipulating figures on spreadsheets, thinking about a PowerPoint presentation, and wondering why his life was so intolerably tedious. But then an email pinged into his inbox. Subject: Stationery Cupboard. A naughty grin spread across Jonathan's face. As he got up from his desk, his mobile buzzed: Alice was calling. But he didn't hesitate: he let the phone go to voicemail, while he went directly to the cupboard where Jane was waiting for him.

'I have a secret for you,' Jane said to Jonathan, her hot breath on his neck as she leaned in, 'about the quarterly earnings.'

'Oh, my, God,' Jonathan replied, in a husky whisper. 'I . . . want . . . you . . . to make some tea with me.'

Get your mind out of the gutter, you smutty muffins: Jonathan is not cheating on Alice. There's a lot more to office relationships than illicit shagging of one's colleagues. In fact, in an age when we are more likely than ever to have colleagues of the opposite sex with whom we work closely and are on the same level of the hierarchy, the more often we find ourselves developing emotionally intimate – but not sexually intimate – relationships with our opposite-sex colleagues. It's unequivocal: the twenty-first century is the age of the office marriage.

A full-time job means that you're spending about a quarter of your life at work, which is a lot of time to exist without someone to serve as a partner in crime, emotional sponge, tea-making companion and best pal . . . all the essential, albeit non-sexual, things that your partner provides for you when he or she is around.

What exactly defines an office marriage? Your office spouse is your best friend in the office. You definitely fancy each other, in that 'I would . . .' kind of way, but you both are dedicated to pretending that it is absolutely not the case, because one or both of you is committed to someone outside the office. And because, as everyone knows, having an actual office romance is probably quite dangerous and irresponsible (skip ahead to the next section now if you need that explained).

You banter constantly, via email or illicit messaging – having an office spouse is so much easier in the information age, when you can be gossiping non-stop without having to do anything that gives your game away, like getting up from your desk to hover near the water cooler. But when you get the chance, you hole up in each other's offices, slurping bad tea and gossiping about your co-workers. When you have a little professional victory, your office spouse is the person you tell first (often before your actual spouse); when something terrible happens, your office spouse hands you tissues and strokes your ego.

You have the same office enemies and office friends (although none of the latter are as special as you are to each other) and you share countless in-jokes and inappropriate bouts of hysterical, snorting laughter in important meetings. When either of you is told anything work-related in confidence, you immediately rush back to your desk to share it with the other. At workplace social events, you spend most of the time chatting to each other in a corner and most of your colleagues think that you are having an affair. But if you ever discuss that particular rumour in one of your frequent intimate chats, you agree that it is a hilarious, appalling prospect . . . even though, you know, under the right circumstances, you would.

And even though an office culture in which these kinds of office marriages are easily facilitated feels quite new, the office marriage itself is quite possibly a sign that we are returning to our evolutionary roots. My consultant primatologist informs me that baboons and macaques, which are thought to be the evolutionary predecessors of early humans, because of similarities in their lifestyles, kind of have office wives too. Amongst these monkeys, males and females that have sex aren't friends, and males and females that are friends don't tend to have sex – the male monkeys groom and hang out with certain monkey ladies, but when it comes to sexy times, like mating season, they don't get together with the ones they hang out with. See? Having an office spouse makes perfect sense: an opportunity to establish a high level of emotional intimacy with someone who you're not having sex with. It is especially important to remember not to have sex with your office spouse, however, even more so than it is important for you not to sleep with your boss: having established that intense emotional intimacy, sex will mean that the two of you either have to get married *tout de suite* or you can never speak again.

I think I love you, but maybe I've just breathed in too many Tipp-Ex fumes.

Oh, but some people can't just stop at being office-married, can they? You'll recall in the early chapter on cohabiting I defined one of the key reasons that we tend to develop crushes on our opposite-sex (platonic) flatmates as the Ice-Dancing Factor, which is what comes into play when a combination of proximity, boredom, and loneliness fuels attraction. Such, I fear, is also often the case with the office romance, although I accept the argument that it will also be more likely to be fuelled by the fact that you and your colleagues probably have at least similar interests as a result of working together, even though the similar interests may be primarily 'hating the boss' and 'loathing the job' and 'really enjoying the turnip that they serve in the canteen on Tuesdays'. Indeed, under these circumstances, it is far from surprising that a mutual state of fancying will follow, and in some cases this can lead to beautiful enduring love affairs which culminate in the two of you having a beautiful wedding in the pub round the corner from the office where you first got drunk together at someone's leaving do, and naming your first child after your employer's best-selling product.

But, alas, such happy conclusions are the exception, rather than the rule: around half of us admit to having got up to some form of hanky-panky with a colleague over the course of our careers. Because of the frequency with which we indulge, the odds that we will end up living happily ever after with our colleagues are, alas, a lot smaller than the odds that we will cringe every time we see them in a staff meeting and wonder why their emails to us always seem to be tinged with the kind of vitriol and disdain that seems out of sync with a discussion about the layout of the company's annual report.

As a trope, office romance is quite an interesting measure of how far we've come since the twentieth century. Initially, the best thing about falling in love with someone at the office was, for women, that (ideally, unless they were the secretary having some kind of bit-on-the-side thing with their married boss) it meant that they could stop working and marry him. Thus the question of whether you could have an affair with someone, though still possibly controversial, was a little less grey because people who got involved with their colleagues didn't expect that the co-working would last particularly long. Post-feminism, when more women worked outside the home than ever before, more office romances blossomed that didn't culminate in the female colleague assuming the role of happy homemaker, but the relative consistency with which women were relegated to subordinate roles meant that the complications of inter-hierarchical loving only went in one direction: women didn't have to ponder whether it was OK to sleep with their deputy or assistant, because there was rarely a chance that the deputy or assistant would be an attractive man.

But, of course, this has not been the case for some time. Even though gender politics in the office have never been so complex as they are now, most of us know that we should know better than to cross lines that should only be crossed with people upon whom you are not dependent in any way for a paycheque. But that fails to prevent us from falling in love or lust, or something that approximates love or lust, with someone who we've only actually ever beheld under the beauty-draining glow of fluorescent lightbulbs. Of course, with the opportunity to constantly communicate with people without leaving your desk or even speaking on the phone, office flirtations have become much easier than the days when one could only hit on a colleague by actually lurking until they walked past the water cooler or getting a secretary to draft a memo to the effect that you would like to take them out for dinner. Now our impressive IT systems mean that situations that perhaps should remain unromantic can become quite saucy very quickly, without due consideration of the potential consequences.

Despite the fact that so many of us pursue office-based romances with frequency and apparent enthusiasm, the consequences of it being discovered remain quite serious – with the seriousness often weighted against the female half of the dangerous office liaison. Putting aside companies with draconian policies that require everyone to actually get sacked if they are caught falling in love, the woman who engages in an office romance and gets caught (and, let's face it, we generally either get caught or break up with our office paramour because of the stress of keeping the relationship under wraps) will most often gain a reputation for being unprofessional . . . or for being the office bicycle. In contrast, quite often the status of the man she was caught shagging on the photocopier (I've never quite understood why people do this. Doesn't it cause the printing toner to get in unmentionable places? That stuff is really hard to clean!) will likely not be negatively affected. Rather he will often be on the receiving end of a bit of congratulatory back-slapping, since the nefarious sexual double standard is certainly not left at the office threshold.

As a result, if you are female and find yourself in a situation where office romance is in the offing, chances are that splashing about in the office inkwell means that you, rather than your partner in the splashing, will be more in danger of negative career outcomes. Thus you may find that you are bit more pressured to hesitate than you might be if you were male. You must take a deep breath and ask yourself the difficult questions: is this gentleman really special enough that I should risk my career over him? Or do I really just fancy him because my job is boring and he is around a lot and whatever deodorant he uses has quite a nice mountain-fresh scent? Am I really prepared to wear a scarf to the office on the hottest day of the summer, after we drink too much champagne at my boss's fiftieth birthday party and he chews on my neck like a sexually uninitiated fifteen-year-old?

I think that the chances are high that the answer to all of those questions is not favourable to romance, in which case I suggest you should gently wheel yourself away from him on your desk chair. If your office paramour is so exceptional that you decide that he is worth risking your career for, you might be wise to consider lining up a new job before you actually allow things to progress, just in case it doesn't all go according to plan, either with you and your new love interest or your company's attitude towards the two of you being in love (yes, it is legal for employment contracts to include clauses that make sleeping with your co-workers an offence that is grounds for termination).

Now let me share with you a morality tale that we all might be wise to keep in mind when we are being distracted by a colleague who seems to be of particular palatability. It is about a young man I met recently, called Angus, and the serious consequences of over-indulging in office romance. Although Angus appeared in many respects to be a fellow of good nature and reasonable moral right-eousness, he made one of the most cardinal errors that one can make when it comes to romancing co-workers: within a matter of weeks, he slept with two of his colleagues. When he told me about it, he did so with what I believe was an air of genuine surprise about the outcome. Angus simply couldn't understand why the women in question, having found out that he was spreading his love so gener-ously throughout the office, had ceased to regard him with warmth. Instead, they were now regarding him with open hostility. 'I don't understand why they hate me,' he said to me, with a plaintive sigh. 'They both seemed happy at the time when we slept together, and it seemed like they knew that it was nothing serious, but now they look daggers at me every time I walk past and are trying to sabotage my project.'

Angus was perhaps not much different from many of his male peers in terms of his capacity to disconnect sex from emotion, thus feeling no particular compunction about having sexual encounters with the women within a short period of time. It is not impossible, of course, for a woman to have a similar attitude to sex. But it tends to take a bit more effort – a degree of effort which the women in question perhaps found unsustainable when they were confronted not only by the spectre of Angus, but by each other, on a daily basis.

Anyone who has ever spent time crying in the office loo knows that in an ideal world, the office should be a sort of emotionless void; while this can rarely be achieved, it is nice if you are not distracted from your spreadsheets and presentations by constant reminders of sexual humiliation. The only thing more distracting from work than an office romance is the fall-out after an office romance: breaking up is hard enough to do without daily being confronted by the spectre of the person who broke your heart (remember, we're supposed to have no contact for a while at least) and to have to treat them with something approaching dignity and respect.

It is nearly impossible and can start to really interfere with your job, whether it is because you are busy scheming for small, secret ways to get revenge by ruining your erstwhile paramour's career (seriously, it is a great way to get sacked, so do step away from his computer, please) or because the person that you dumped is now sending evil glares at you on an hourly basis and interfering with your filing cabinets. Or sometimes it can just interfere because even though both of you are trying to behave with the utmost dignity, your ears are burning from the sound of everyone gossiping about what happened between the two of you, watching you hawkishly during board meetings in an attempt to detect tension or heartbreak or shreds of remaining affection – because, frankly, there are few offices where someone else's workplace affair is not more interesting than the actual work that needs to be done.

My rule of thumb? If you are going to have a sexy relationship with a colleague at some point during your employment at a particular company, probably best to regard it as a sort of Get-Out-Of-Jail-Free card in the

Monopoly game of life: whether you are male or female you can get away with doing it once, but anything more frequent will mean that you are really pushing your luck, unless you have already taken the time to put together a CV that is even more seductive than the colleagues you have loved and lost.

In summary:

Himglish: Women have jobs too. Sometimes, they make more money than you, or are even your boss! In fact, it can be fun.

Femalese: Despite major advancements in gender equity, the world of work remains one in which women remain frequently compromised. Thus they must often consider their actions, especially when it comes to crossing the lines between the professional and the personal, in a different light to their male counterparts.

The End

How are you feeling? A little worn out? I've bombarded you with a lot of information and a lot of food for thought, I realise. I'm exhausted, too. But the exhaustion is worth it, because you've acquired a grip of some basic key principles for getting along with the opposite sex in this wild new era.

Looking ahead, thinking about how you are going to apply what we have learned here, everything may not be perfectly clear. But that is totally OK: I never said that this would be easy, or that you would be able to change your life instantly, or even that you would have to. But now that you realise how your lack of comprehension of the opposite sex parallels their incomprehension of you, then maybe – just maybe – might you be able to feel a bit more positive, a bit less defeated, by the difficult prospect of being a woman living with men (or a man, living with women) in the twenty-first century? I think so.

If you have learned nothing else from this treatise, I hope that it will be that there is ultimately no point in wringing your hands and declaiming that there is no way on earth that we shall ever be able to get along because we are too different. Yes, we are different, but now that we have accepted and acknowledged that, we can no longer use the fact that we are mystified as an excuse for treating each other with anything less than the kind of dignity that we would require ourselves – or with which we would treat members of the same sex as us who we believe we do understand.

And, at the same time, it is important to remember that not only is it OK that we don't totally comprehend the opposite sex, sometimes it's kind of great. Sure, Alice could speak exclusively in Himglish and Jonathan could become totally proficient at speaking Femalese, but the result would be that they would no longer be themselves.

Alice:	I want you to love me unconditionally. That is exactly what I want you to do. Now I will carefully enumerate the reasons why I love you. It will take hours.
Jonathan:	I have noticed the subtle non-verbal messages you are sending and I'd just like you to know that I feel exactly the same about you.

How atrocious. They'd be dull, their relationship would fail to be spicy. Alice and Jonathan would either devote themselves to welding and cake-decorating and never have sex again, or they would be compelled to seek out new partners who they didn't quite understand – because, ultimately, though we find each other frustrating, part of the reason that men and women are so drawn to each other is that things that are mystifying and exotic and strange and inexplicable are, well, fascinating. It sounds terribly trite, but diversity truly is a beautiful thing.

Your mission from here on in, which I am not giving you a choice but am rather compelling you to accept, is that you make an effort out there, henceforth, to be kind, to be patient, and to be dynamic enough that you can accept that many interactions between men and women resemble a balanced equation much less than they do a tennis match between two players with limited ball control. Once you stop fighting entropy, I think you may be surprised just how much things happen, despite everything, to fall into place.

Alice: Jonathan, you are totally weird, but I love you anyway.

Jonathan: And despite your oddness, I love you right back.

Get it? Good.

In summary . . .

Himglish: The end.

Femalese: The end.

Acknowledgements

First and foremost, thanks to the team at Preface: my editor, Trevor Dolby, deserves the most gratitude, as well as Nicola Taplin and Stephen Dumughn. Thanks also to my publicist, Annabel Robinson, the team at FMcM and everyone else at Random House.

Huge thanks to Stephanie Thwaites – long before she was my literary agent, she was one of my dearest friends. She is a star.

Thanks also to the following people, who have been early readers and/or suppliers of anecdotes, cheerleaders, editors, mentors, employers, encouragers, consultant primatologists, photographers, gay husbands, platonic life partners, neighbours, flatmates, web designers, BFFs: Christiane Bode, Lauren Brent, Benjamin S. Buckland, Jude Bunting, Ross Carroll, Ryan Gessner, Benjamin Harrison, Olivia Laing, Lydia Lewis, Julia Margo, Alex Marquez, Hetty Marriott-Brittan, Jodie Marsh, Alyssa McDonald, Sebastian Meyer, Rebecca Molinoff, Lucy Murray, Christine Palmer, Jack Roberts, Justin Sherin, Sonia Sodha, Daniel Stacey, Anastasya Partan Tveteraas, Niels Weise, Rebecca Young. You are all lovely.

And finally, tremendous thanks are due to my family. Fiona, William, Arthur D. and Elspeth Edelstein, Arthur S. Edelstein and Dorleau Roth, and the late Jane Jones, all of whom have been nothing but supportive and encouraging and inspiring for the whole of my life.